The Assault on Evangelical Support for Israel

CAMERA Monograph Series

A publication of CAMERA,
Committee for Accuracy in Middle East Reporting in America
Boston, Massachusetts

CAMERA, the Committee for Accuracy in Middle East Reporting in America, is a national media-monitoring organization founded in 1982 that works to promote more accurate, balanced and complete coverage of Israel and the Middle East. Aware of the vital role of the mass media in shaping public perception and public policy, CAMERA seeks to educate both journalists and news consumers about the complex issues related to achievement of peace in the Middle East. CAMERA is a non-profit, tax-exempt organization under section 501(c)(3) of the United States Internal Revenue Code.

Published by
The Committee for Accuracy in Middle East Reporting in America
CAMERA
P.O. Box 35040
Boston, MA 02135

ISBN 978-0-9661548-8-7

Book design: Emily Regan

Cover image: flash90

Photos: commons.wikipedia.org with the following exceptions: P. 14 Scan from cover of program, P. 15, 16 Christ at the Checkpoint Young Adult Conference promotional video screen capture, P. 16 scan from cover of movie, P. 17 scans from E21 Program, P. 18 Dexter Van Zile, P. 19 oruoracle.com, P. 21 Dexter Van Zile, P. 22 *With God on Our Side* screen capture, P. 23 scan from cover of movie P. 25 *Little Town of Bethlehem* screen capture, P. 29 (Mitri Raheb) Dexter Van Zile, P. 31 scan from cover of program, P. 63 oikoumene.org, P. 66 Dexter Van Zile, P. 67 etrfi.org P. 72 loc.gov

CONTENTS

Forward 7

Introduction 9
Andrea Levin, Executive Director CAMERA

Foundations of the Christian Anti-Israel Agenda 11

Significant Developments in the Assault on Evangelical Support for Israel 13
Tricia Miller, Ph.D.

The New Church Struggle 20
Dexter Van Zile

The *Kairos Palestine Document*, Anti-Israel Boycotts, and How to Combat Them 28
Malcolm Lowe

Antidotes for the Threat to Evangelical Support for Israel 35

Countering the Threats to Evangelical Support of Israel 37
Laurie Cardoza-Moore, Th.M.

The Case for Israel 43
Shadi Khalloul

Why Should Christians Be Zionists? 51
Rev. Gerald R. McDermott, Ph.D.

Antidote for the Threat to Evangelical Support of Israel:
A Renewal of Leadership within the Church 62
Rev. Petra Heldt, Ph.D.

Compelling Reasons for Jewish-Evangelical Cooperation in Support of Israel 69

The Jewish Roots of Christianity 71
Brad H. Young, Ph.D.

Jewish-Christian Relations and Cooperation for Israel 82
Rabbi Yitzchok Adlerstein

A Reason for Hope: Christians United for Israel 86
Randal Neal

Appendices 89

Empowered 21 and Christians Who Promote Anti-Israel Propaganda 91
Tricia Miller, Ph.D.

Empowered21 Threatens Jewish-Christian Relations 93
Tricia Miller, Ph.D.

Where are Empowered21 and Oral Roberts University Headed in Relation to Israel? 95
Tricia Miller, Ph.D.

CAMERA Asks Mart Green to Unwind Damage to Israel's Reputation by *Little Town of Bethlehem* 100
Dexter Van Zile

A New Christian Zionism: Understanding Supersessionism and Why It Is Unbiblical 120
Gerald R. McDermott, Ph.D.

Forward

CAMERA convened an all day international conference in Los Angeles on January 18, 2016 to examine the roots and effects of a well-orchestrated assault on Evangelical support for Israel. The event provided the more than 200 attendees with resources to counter the anti-Zionist agenda, and presented compelling reasons for continued cooperation between Jews and Evangelicals in support of Israel. The overwhelmingly positive response from Jewish and Christian attendees demonstrated the importance of addressing this critical subject.

Evangelical Christians are the latest focus of an aggressive and deceptive pro-Palestinian/anti-Israel campaign designed to turn traditional supporters of Israel away from that support in favor of the Palestinian cause. The effort to turn Evangelical support away from the Jewish State is spearheaded by Palestinian Christians, and is advanced by Christian leaders in the West who not only support the Palestinian cause, but help promote its anti-Zionist message to an extensive audience in the US and around the world.

Evangelical support for Israel is based on a historic and theological foundation that is as old as Christianity. Ever since the beginnings of the Evangelical movement – which predates the founding of the State of Israel by over two hundred years – Evangelicals have believed that Jews have the right to re-establish a nation in their ancient homeland. It is precisely because of this historic belief that the Evangelical base of support for Israel has become the object of a politically motivated crusade, disguised in Christian terms, that targets unsuspecting Evangelicals with an emotionally-laden message rooted in revisionist history and erroneous theology.

The flawed theology that forms the foundation of the Palestinian political narrative is a customized version of an almost 2000-year-old replacement theology, which maintains that Christians and the Church have replaced Jews and Israel in the purposes of God. Palestinian replacement theology replaces Jews and Israel through the false claim that Palestinians are the indigenous people of the land. This rewritten history concludes that Palestinians are the rightful owners of the land and the Jewish State is illegitimate.

This monograph contains material from the conference in Los Angeles that exposes the politically motivated, religious crusade to delegitimize Israel. It is published with two goals in mind. The first is to equip Evangelicals with the information necessary to refute the faulty narrative at the heart of the Palestinian Christian anti-Israel message. The second objective is to negate the threat Christian anti-Zionism poses to Evangelical-Jewish relations by encouraging Evangelicals and Jews to continue their collaboration for the sake of Israel.

The initial chapters of this volume name particular individuals and institutions responsible for the promotion of the Palestinian Christian narrative. Identification of the perpetrators of the anti-Zionist campaign is necessary in order to enable Evangelicals to counter the assault at its source.

Early chapters also discuss various aspects of the revisionist history and fallacious theology that form the foundation of the Palestinian political agenda. This too is essential in order to inoculate Evangelicals against the deception upon which the movement is founded.

Subsequent chapters provide antidotes to the efforts to undermine Evangelical support for Israel. A first-hand description of life as an Israeli Christian, and an examination of the reasons Christians should be Zionists, provide important resources in the battle for truth. Concrete methodologies are presented that, if implemented, will work to secure future Evangelical support for the Jewish state. Insightful discussions of the Jewish roots of Christianity and the importance of the pursuit of justice provide compelling reasons for Jewish-Evangelical cooperation in support of Israel.

Because of the effects of the ongoing assault on Evangelical support for Israel, this historic source of advocacy for the Jewish homeland can no longer be taken for granted.

However, there is still reason for hope. Millions of Evangelicals remain dedicated supporters of Israel, and are affiliated with organizations such as Christians United for Israel and Proclaiming Justice to the Nations, both of which were represented at the conference in Los Angeles. Providing these advocates with the facts will enable them to stand firm against the anti-Zionist intent to undermine Evangelical support for the Jewish State.

Andrea Levin
Executive Director, CAMERA

Introduction

Andrea Levin, Executive Director CAMERA

Andrea Levin is the Executive Director and President of CAMERA, the organization she has directed for 25 years. Ms. Levin, who was named in 2003 by the *Forward* newspaper as one of the most influential American Jews, writes and lectures widely on media coverage of the Arab-Israeli conflict and its impact on public opinion. Her columns have appeared in numerous publications, including the *Wall Street Journal, Jerusalem Post, Boston Globe, International Herald Tribune, New York Post, New Republic, Middle East Quarterly, National Post* and *Commentary.*

We were delighted to see a significant turnout for an important event in Los Angeles, sponsored by CAMERA to focus on extremely urgent issues related to Israel and to the bonds between Jews and Evangelical Christians.

CAMERA is a 35-year-old organization with 65,000 members around the world. We're based in Boston with offices in New York, Los Angeles, Palm Beach, Washington DC and Jerusalem. CAMERA is the pioneer and leader in monitoring media coverage of Israel and the Middle East. We work to promote accurate coverage through systematic attention to reporting, fact-checking, intensive interaction with journalists, editors, producers and executives – and engagement of the voices of our nearly 20,000 activists.

We believe there are objective truths in current affairs, in history, and in matters related to our shared Judeo-Christian heritage.

We focus not only on whether media outlets such as *The New York Times* and CNN get the facts right about events in the Arab-Israeli conflict, but for three decades we've also worked to promote accurate information in Christian media, including publications, documentaries, books, websites and proclamations.

CAMERA does not take political positions on American or Israeli governmental policies or advocate for or against any official or political actions. Our staff, boards and membership span the political spectrum, but they are united in the belief that distortions and outright lies about Israel fuel conflict and hatred and should be opposed at every turn.

We advocate for factual media coverage – for complete, balanced rendition of the realities. We believe there are objective truths in current affairs, in history, and in matters related to our shared Judeo-Christian heritage, despite the twisted and seemingly bizarre assertions of some who may seek to destroy the bonds of Jews and their Christian allies. For example, the fact is, Jesus was not a Palestinian. He was a Jew. Incredibly, this is a matter that potentially looms large and we'll learn more later about the reason.

Lord Arthur Balfour

We at CAMERA, and many in the Jewish community, are fully aware of the long history of Christian Zionism and the many historic figures in the Evangelical world who have worked, some heroically, on Israel's behalf. Lord Arthur Balfour spelled out British support for the restoration of a Jewish homeland. General Orde

Wingate passionately spoke out for the Jews in the 1930's, believing in the cause on religious, political and moral grounds.

Colonel John Patterson commanded the Jewish Legion in World War I and was a lifelong Zionist. He and his wife died here in California some years ago and their wish was to be interred in Israel near some of the fighters he'd once led. In 2014, their remains were moved to a moshav north of Netanya founded by members of the Jewish Legion.

Many, many other Christian Zionists have stood by the side of Israel in her hour of need. The bonds extend back into the past and are powerful today too. But at a time when the Jewish state is under a widespread propaganda assault there are troubling signs some of the lies about Israel have begun to affect the attitudes and beliefs of some in this important community.

Our meeting in Los Angeles was just the first step in exploring and exposing the potential damage to Israel and to the Evangelical alliance with Israel that needs to be understood and reversed. We are now distributing this monograph containing material from the conference, and we are holding similar events in other cities in the U.S. Our goal is to halt defamation of Israel where it's occurring and to protect the precious alliance of Jews and Evangelical Christians.

Our speakers in LA were leading experts on a range of issues related to the subject of Evangelical support for Israel. We heard first from Dr. Tricia Miller who is a Senior Research Analyst with CAMERA. She monitors Christian organizations and media activity in relation to the Arab-Israeli conflict. She has been published in numerous publications including *First Things, The Algemeiner, New English Review, Charisma News, Breaking Israel News, Times of Israel, JNS,* and the *Jerusalem Post.*

Tricia has a Ph.D. in the Hebrew Bible and wrote her dissertation on anti-Semitism in relation to the book of Esther. Her book, *Jews and Anti-Judaism in Esther and the Church,* was published in May 2015, and addresses the relationship of Esther to current Christian anti-Judaism and anti-Zionism. Tricia presented very important information about why we're alarmed about trends in the Evangelical world.

Foundations of the Christian Anti-Israel Agenda

Significant Developments in the Assault on Evangelical Support for Israel

Tricia Miller, Ph.D.

Dr. Tricia Miller is a Christian Media Analyst for CAMERA. She monitors Christian organizations and media in relation to the Arab-Israeli conflict and focuses specifically on the effects of Christian anti-Zionism on support for Israel in the Evangelical world. Her book, *Jews and Anti-Judaism in Esther and the Church,* addresses the relationship of the Book of Esther to current Christian anti-Judaism and anti-Zionism.

Our program for the conference in Los Angeles included leading scholars and religious leaders who examined various aspects of the assault on Evangelical support for Israel, provided antidotes for this anti-Zionist crusade, and presented compelling reasons for Jewish-Evangelical cooperation in support of Israel. Our hope is that the material presented in the following chapters will inform, equip and inspire Evangelicals and Jews to work together for the sake of truth in relation to Israel.

It is precisely because of this historic belief in a Jewish homeland that the Evangelical base of support for Israel has become the target of an increasingly successful political campaign, disguised in theological terms.

I want to introduce three recent developments that represent significant threats to the future of Evangelical support for Israel. These developments already play, or have the potential to play, a major role in a politically motivated crusade that targets American Evangelicals for the purpose of winning spiritual and financial support for the Palestinian cause. But before I begin, I want to give a brief explanation of the theological underpinnings of the concerted effort to turn the Evangelical world away from Israel.

Theological Foundation of the Assault

Evangelical support for Israel is based on a historic and theological foundation that is as old as Christianity. Ever since the beginnings of the Evangelical movement – which predates the founding of the State of Israel by a couple of hundred years – Evangelicals have believed that Jews have the right to re-establish a nation in their ancient homeland. It is precisely because of this historic belief in a Jewish homeland that the Evangelical base of support for Israel has become the target of an increasingly successful political campaign, disguised in theological terms.

Palestinian replacement theology replaces Jews in the purposes of God through the outrageous claim that Palestinians are the indigenous people of the Land.

The crusade to gain support for the Palestinian cause is clothed in a false theological and historical narrative that appeals to well-meaning Christians who are moved by an emotional message that lacks facts, historical context, and a consistent method of biblical interpretation. The erroneous theology and rewritten history that forms the foundation of the Palestinian political narrative is nothing more than a customized version of 2000-year-old replacement theology, which maintains that Christians and the Church have replaced Jews and Israel in the purposes of God.

Palestinian replacement theology replaces Jews in the purposes of God through the outrageous claim that Palestinians are the indigenous people of the Land. According to this belief, the Jews who now live in Israel are of European descent and only appeared in the Land in the 19th century. Therefore, Palestinians are the rightful owners of the Land and they are being oppressed by illegal occupiers. In other words, the Jewish State is illegitimate.

The assertion that Palestinians have owned the Land for 2000 years promotes a political cause, but it also has other far-reaching ramifications. The logical conclusion of the claim that Palestinians are indigenous to the Land is the belief that Jesus was a Palestinian. After all, how could Jesus have been Jewish if there were no Jews in the Land when he was born there? This is in fact what many Palestinian Christians believe, and there are serious consequences from this politically inspired theology.

The logical conclusion of the claim that Palestinians are indigenous to the Land is the belief that Jesus was a Palesinian.

The invention of a Palestinian Jesus denies the Jewishness of Jesus and deconstructs the foundations of Christian faith by severing that faith from its Jewish roots and context. As a result, the Christian faith is delegitimized. A Palestinian Jesus is also dangerous for Jews. When Jesus is separated from his Jewishness, the way is paved for the same demonization and dehumanization of the Jewish people that resulted from the Nazi's identification of Jesus as an Aryan. And we know from history where this road leads.

Significant Developments in the Assault

With this explanation of the theological underpinnings of this politically motivated movement in mind, I want to discuss three significant developments that threaten future Evangelical support of Israel – all of which began in 2010.

Christ at the Checkpoint Conferences

2010 was the year the first in a series of conferences known as Christ at the Checkpoint was held in Bethlehem. Since 2010, this gathering has been hosted every two years by Bethlehem Bible College, which is an Evangelical Christian college. The president of the school is a man by the name of Jack Sara. Through the outreach of this school, American Evangelicals are targeted with a one-sided message that is based on Palestinian replacement theology, fallacious charges of racism and apartheid, and a flawed historical narrative. The majority of the participants at Christ at the Checkpoint conferences are American Evangelical leaders who return to the US and propagate a narrative that is nothing more than Christian anti-Zionism, which is the new manifestation of Christian anti-Semitism.

It is important to note that through content and imagery, these Palestinian Christians promote a very clear message – Israelis are oppressing them in the same way first century Jews allegedly persecuted Christ. The implication is that if Jesus lived in Bethlehem today, he would have to go through checkpoints just like the Palestinians do – because remember, according to them, Jesus was a Palestinian. In reality, Jesus would not be allowed into the Bethlehem of today – not because of the Israelis, but because of the Palestinian Authority, which has declared that all territory under their control must be *Judenrein*.

The majority of the participants at Christ at the Checkpoint conferences are American Evangelical leaders who return to the US and propagate a narrative that is nothing more than Christian anti-Zionism.

This reality leads me to point out an obvious, glaring inconsistency in the Palestinian narrative. On one hand, the claim is made that Jesus was a Palestinian, since according to their political script, there were no Jews in the land 2000 years ago. On the other hand, the message from Bethlehem Bible College and Christ at the Checkpoint is that if Jesus lived there today, he would be oppressed by the Israelis in the same way he was persecuted by first century Jews.

But how could Jesus have been persecuted by Jews if they weren't there when he was there? Which is it? Were there Jews in the land 2000 years ago or not? Unfortunately, this propaganda doesn't let facts or standard methods of biblical interpretation get in the way. What is important for the sake of the Palestinian narrative is the perpetuation of the two millennia-old Christian canard that says Jews persecute Christians.

In addition to its conferences, Christ at the Checkpoint spreads its anti-Israel message through videos made available on YouTube.

In addition to its conferences, Christ at the Checkpoint spreads its anti-Israel message through videos made available on YouTube. In March of 2015, this organization produced a two-minute piece promoting an upcoming Christ at the Checkpoint Young Adult Conference that provides a graphic example of just how vile Christian anti-Zionism can get.

Through graphic footage, this video equates Israel's anti-terrorist security measures with the atrocities ISIS commits. Images of ISIS captives about to be beheaded are juxtaposed with images of Israel's security wall. Images of the Jordanian pilot about to be burned alive in a cage are juxtaposed with people behind bars going through a checkpoint. And images of the ISIS flag are juxtaposed with images of the Israeli flag. The video also equates ISIS and Israel with the H1N1 virus, also known as the Swine flu, which, as we know, is highly contagious.

Jordanian Pilot burned alive by ISIS

Palestinian Checkpoint

One can only conclude that the producers of this video are comparing the existence of Israel – or at the very least, the existence of the security barrier and the need for checkpoints – with the contagious spread of swine flu and the ease with which ISIS conquers territory and the savagery with which it terrorizes its victims. Not to mention what appears to be the obvious analogy between the Jewish State and a virus named for pigs. This is just one of a number of

Shot of ISIS Flag in Christ at the Checkpoint video

Shot of Israeli Flag in Christ at the Checkpoint video

highly offensive and dangerous videos produced by Christ at the Checkpoint and its sponsoring institution, Bethlehem Bible College – both of which are under the leadership of President Jack Sara.

Anti-Israel Christian Documentaries

The second significant development of 2010 was the production of a virulently anti-Israel Christian documentary, titled *Little Town of Bethlehem.* This documentary was produced by Mart Green (one of the owners of the retail chain, Hobby Lobby) under the direction of Sami Awad of the Holy Land Trust. The Holy Land Trust is a pro-Palestinian organization headquartered in Bethlehem that also helps sponsor Christ at the Checkpoint conferences.

This film presents a false narrative...and is nothing more than propaganda that demonizes and delegitimizes the Jewish State.

In short, this film presents a false narrative consistent with that of Christ at the Checkpoint, and is nothing more than propaganda that demonizes and delegitimizes the Jewish State. It has been shown in over four hundred venues across the US, including Evangelical college campuses and Evangelical churches. As a result, it has made a significant contribution to the promotion of the Palestinian agenda and the undermining of the next generation of Evangelical support for Israel.

Publicity photo for the 2010 movie *Little Town of Bethlehem*

In the next chapter, Dexter Van Zile, will go into much more detail on the particular problems associated with this movie. But, *Little Town of Bethlehem* needed to be mentioned at this point because of its relevance to the third significant development of 2010, which was the year a new worldwide organization called Empowered21 held its first international conference in Tulsa, OK.

Empowered21

Empowered21's stated vision is "That every person on Earth would have an authentic encounter with Jesus Christ through the Power and Presence of the Holy Spirit by Pentecost 2033." According to this organization, in order for their mission to be accomplished, Evangelical Christians worldwide must be united.

JERUSALEM 2015
EMPOWERED21 GLOBAL CONGRESS

I attended Empowered21's international conference this past May in Jerusalem. Every speaker in the main sessions, over the course of 4 days – morning, afternoon and night – in some way emphasized the necessity of Christian unity in order to realize the goal of world evangelization.

There is a twofold problem with this call to unity. The first is that no definition was given by any of the speakers as to what the leadership of Empowered21 means by their use of the word "unity." As a result, the probability is that conference attendees will interpret this call according to the dictionary definition of unity, which is "the state of being in full agreement." In other words, unity requires agreement.

It appears that Empowered21 is calling Evangelicals to stand in unity with those who promote a political narrative that demonizes Jews, and delegitimizes the Jewish State.

Second, in the absence of any other definition or parameters for this unity, and in light of Empowered 21's unreflective support for, and involvement with, Palestinian Christian leaders, as demonstrated in Jerusalem in May, it appears that Empowered21 is calling Evangelicals to stand in unity with those who promote a political narrative that demonizes Jews, and delegitimizes the Jewish State.

Empowered21's relationship with Palestinian Christians is demonstrated in part, by the inclusion of Jack Sara, president of Bethlehem Bible College, as one of the leaders in the conference in Jerusalem.

This emphasis on unity at the expense of truth...means that Empowered21 could well become a vehicle for the international promotion of the Palestinian Christian anti-Zionist narrative.

As president of Bethlehem Bible College, Sara is not only responsible for the college's promotion of Palestinian replacement theology and anti-Israel propaganda, but he is responsible for the way this school targets the American Evangelical audience with its message.

Furthermore, Jack Sara is responsible for the anti-Zionist message promoted at Christ at the Checkpoint conferences, which are sponsored by his Bible College. And, he is responsible for the videos produced by Christ at the Checkpoint, such as the promotional clip that equates Israel with ISIS. His involvement in Empowered21 suggests that a Christian with these beliefs is to be included among those with whom Empowered21 advocates unity or, "the state of being in full agreement."

Jack Sara, President, Bethlehem Bible college

But, how can Evangelicals stand in unity with those who promote a political agenda built on a foundation of lies, rewritten history and anti-Jewish theology? How can Evangelicals, who claim to believe what the Bible says, also claim to be in unity with those who reinvent Jesus as a Palestinian, deny the Jewish roots of Christianity, and maintain that Christians and the Church have replaced Jews and Israel in the purposes of God?

This emphasis on unity at the expense of truth – as evidenced by the relationships between leaders of Empowered21 and Palestinian leaders such as Jack Sara – means that Empowered21 could well become a vehicle for the international promotion of the Palestinian Christian anti-Zionist narrative. This would represent the most extensive threat to Evangelical support of Israel we have seen yet, simply because of the worldwide reach of Empowered21.

Connections Between the Three Developments

At this point, I want to provide some more data points to illustrate the connections between the three significant developments in the assault on Evangelical support of Israel since 2010 – Christ at the Checkpoint conferences, the production of *Little Town of Bethlehem* and the Empowered21 movement.

The chairman of Empowered21 is Dr. Billy Wilson. Wilson was a speaker at the Christ at The Checkpoint conference in March 2014, and Wilson is responsible for the inclusion of Palestinian leaders such as the president of Bethlehem Bible College in Empowered21. Wilson is also the president of Oral Roberts University, an internationally recognized Christian university in Tulsa, OK. Because of this, ORU now plays a significant role in advancing the Empowered21 movement.

Dr. Billy Wilson, President of ORU, speaking at Christ at the Checkpoint.

With that said, I want to make it clear that while the relationship between Billy Wilson, Christ at the Checkpoint, and leaders such as Jack Sara is cause for concern, this reality does not reflect on the many ORU professors who wholeheartedly support Israel and understand the importance of Jewish-Christian relations. Prior to the presidency of Billy Wilson, ORU had an exemplary history of support for Israel, and evidence of ORU's historic position towards Israel is demonstrated by the fact that the vast majority of those still associated with ORU – professors and students alike – understand the importance of standing with Israel.

The concern over the relationship between the leadership of ORU, Empowered21, Bethlehem Bible College and Christ at the Checkpoint is magnified as a result of the relationship between the source of funding for ORU, Empowered21, and the film, *Little Town of Bethlehem.*

However, I have to mention ORU because an understanding of the relationship between the current leadership of the university and the leadership of Bethlehem Bible College and Christ at the Checkpoint is essential in order to understand the danger represented by the goals of Empowered21.

The concern over the relationship between the leadership of ORU, Empowered21, Bethlehem Bible College and Christ at the Checkpoint is magnified as a result of the relationship between the source of funding for ORU, Empowered21, and the film, *Little Town of Bethlehem* – the one that promotes the same anti-Israel propaganda as Bethlehem Bible College and Christ at the Checkpoint. And there is a lot of money involved.

Mart Green, the producer of *Little Town of Bethlehem*, was the chair of the Oral Roberts Board of trustees from 2008-2014. Since 2008, Green has given $250 million to the school – a fact that not only bought him the position of chair of the board, but one that continues to give him an inordinate amount of influence and power. Empowered21 was Mart Green's idea after he became chair of the board and Empowered21 is supported and promoted by the university Mart Green has funded. This is the reason ORU now plays a significant role in the advancement of Empowered21.

Mart Green

Mart Green, of course, is a member of the board of Empowered21 and was a participant in the conference in Jerusalem along with Jack Sara and other pro-Palestinian pastors.

To summarize, in Empowered21, we have the combination of Mart Green's money and influence, his obvious sympathy for the Palestinian Christian narrative, as demonstrated by his production of *Little Town of Bethlehem*, and the relationship of Empowered21 leadership to Palestinian Christian leaders like Jack Sara. This does not bode well in terms of the influence this organization may have on Evangelical support for Israel internationally.

For more detail on my concerns about the potential effects of the Empowered21 movement on the future of Evangelical support for Israel, please see three articles I have written that can be found in the appendices of this book.

In closing, I want to remind us of something we understand from history, and that is, that all it takes for evil to prevail is for good people to remain silent. In the biblical book of Esther, in the context of an impending genocide of the Jews, Mordecai challenged Esther to not remain silent in the face of evil, but to use her position to change the course of history. He also cautioned her that inaction on her part would not insure her safety, even in the King's palace.

May we all heed the message of Mordecai and follow the example of Esther. Let us all continue to speak and stand for the truth in relation to Israel. May we do all we can, where we can, in such a time as this.

The New Church Struggle

Dexter Van Zile

Dexter Van Zile is a Christian Media Analyst for CAMERA. His work has focused on the failure of the World Council of Churches and other Christian institutions to address human rights abuses in Muslim-majority countries in the Middle East. He has also played a major role in exposing the errors in the Palestinian Christian narrative and has made an important contribution in the battle for accuracy in relation to Christian anti-Zionism.

Up until a few years ago, it would have been unthinkable that we would need to have a conference or publish a book about anti-Zionism in the Evangelical community. Evangelicals have been some of Israel's most ardent supporters and for the most part, that is still the case. Polling data indicates that Evangelicals in the United States are more likely than American Jews to believe that God gave the land of Israel to the Jewish people. Support for Israel in the Evangelical community is still robust, but not to be taken for granted.

Up until 2010, anti-Israel activism was a marginal aspect of Evangelical life in the U.S. There was an organization called Evangelicals for Middle East Understanding that blamed the conflict and the suffering it caused on Israel and its Christian Zionist supporters in the U.S. It got some traction, but not a lot.

In 2005, there was a conference at North Park University about the evils of Christian Zionism. The conference's message was that Christian Zionists had embraced a dangerous end time theology that caused people to ignore the suffering of the Palestinian people. Interestingly, the same folks who worry about the end-time beliefs of pre-millennial dispensationalists have said very little about the end-time beliefs of the mullahs in Iran. But you knew that.

The message offered at the conference at North Park was a pretty simple message that resonated with mainline or liberal Protestants and some Evangelicals, but it didn't get much traction in mainstream Evangelicalism. Mainliners, like a lot of people in the United States, had contempt for Evangelicals and they used this contempt to portray Evangelical support for Israel as a retrograde movement.

Anti-Zionism started to get traction within the Evangelical community in 2010. CAMERA raised a hue and a cry about a growing number of disaffected young Evangelicals embracing anti-Zionism as a way to signal their non-Evangelical friends that they were hip, slick and cool, unlike their parents and grandparents.

There are two main pillars of what some commentators have called the Evangelical Intifada. One pillar is the Christ at the Checkpoint Conferences organized by a group of Palestinian Christians associated with Bethlehem Bible College in Bethlehem.

The overarching motif of these conferences, which have been held every even-numbered year beginning in 2010 at a five star hotel in Bethlehem, is displayed in a banner on the stage behind the speakers.

The banner shows a church and a cross standing in opposition to – and in judgment of – a guard tower that sits atop the security barrier. The message is that Israel's security barrier and Jewish sovereignty itself are obstacles to God's purposes for the Holy Land.

Conference speakers portray Christian support for Israel as a betrayal of Christianity's universalism. For example, Dr. Manfred Kohl, a German theologian, argued that Christian support or acknowledgment of Jewish territorial claims were a betrayal of Christianity and of Jesus himself.

"For us today, to insist on holding onto some parts of the old covenant means not to recognize Christ in His totality," he said. This type of argumentation puts Christians who support Israel on the defensive because it forces them to choose between their love of Jesus Christ and of the Jewish people.

The logo for the 2016 Christ at the Checkpoint Conference

Speakers at these conferences and others like them in the U.S. also assert that Christian support for Israel hinders efforts to spread the Christian faith in Muslim-majority countries in the Middle East. The logic is that because Muslims regard Israel with hostility, Evangelical support for Israel puts the Christian faith in a bad light and therefore makes Muslims less likely to convert to Christianity.

Given the importance the Evangelical community places on sharing the faith, this argument hits home in spite of the fact that it ignores the lack of religious freedom in Muslim-majority countries. Speakers also blame Christian support for the Jewish state in the Middle East for the oppression of Christians in the region. This is another effective argument because Evangelicals are some of the most prominent supporters of organizations that advocate for persecuted Christians in the Middle East.

Professor Gary Burge from Wheaton College leading a group of students at the 2016 Christ at the Checkpoint conference.

Students from Wheaton College have attended CATC conferences. They attend under the supervision of Professor Gary Burge, a well-known anti-Israel writer who has proven skillful at enlisting students into the cause of anti-Zionist activism.

In 2012, students from the school spray-painted the message "Wheaton College, For Christ and No Walls" on the security barrier in Bethlehem, demonstrating that they internalized the message of Christ at the Checkpoint logo quite nicely. They condemned the wall, but not the terror attacks that prompted its construction.

High-ranking officials from the World Evangelical Alliance, the umbrella organization for Evangelicals worldwide, have also attended the conference.

George Tunnicliffe, then secretary general of the WEA, was at the 2014 conference, and the new Secretary General Bishop, Efraim Tendero, will attend the next conference taking place this March.

The presence of these officials legitimizes the message offered by CATC.

The second pillar of the Evangelical Intifada are two highly propagandistic movies shown to thousands of college-age Evangelicals at hundreds of college campuses in the United States and Europe. One of these films was *With God on Our Side*, which was released in 2010.

This film, produced by Porter Speakman Jr., shows the struggles of a young Evangelical Christian as he grapples with the continued violence of the Arab-Israeli conflict. He starts out as a Christian supporter of Israel, but by the end he has embraced a narrative that blames Israel for the conflict and downplays incitement and antisemitism in Palestinian society. The movie provides a visual model for young Evangelicals to embrace the anti-Israel narrative.

The protagonist of the 2010 movie *With God on Our Side* struggling with his conscience.

Here's a screenshot of the young Evangelical speaking on camera about his dark night of the soul. You can see the stained glass behind him. It's a very dishonest movie, but as a piece of visual propaganda, it's very effective.

The movie suggests that good Christians can ignore Muslim and Arab hostility toward Jews and Israel because of the crimes the Jewish state has committed against the Palestinian people. I've asked Porter Speakman, Jr. who paid for the production of this movie, but he has never given me the names of the people who bankrolled it.

We do know, however, who paid for another vulgar anti-Israel movie, *Little Town of Bethlehem*. This movie, released in 2010, was produced by Mart Green, an heir to the Hobby Lobby fortune and founder of Mardel, a chain of Christian bookstores.

Mart Green hired a writer who was smitten by Hassan Nasrallah, the leader of one of the most anti-Semitic organizations on the planet to produce a film about the Arab-Israeli conflict. This is simply irresponsible.

This movie is quite simply one of the ugliest examples of anti-Israel propaganda that CAMERA has seen. It is billed as a documentary about nonviolence, but it is actually a salvo in the propaganda war against the Jewish state and ultimately the Jewish people as a whole.

First, some background about the movie. It was written and directed by a former advertising executive, Jim Hanon, who made other movies for Mart Green, which were sold through Mardel's store and website.

In writing the script for the movie, Jim Hanon spent a lot of time with Holy Land Trust, a Bethlehem-based organization led by Sami Awad, who comes from a prominent family of Palestinian Christians who have made a family business of demonizing Israel.

Hanon also visited with Hassan Nasrallah, the Hezbollah leader, a man who once expressed a desire to kill all the Jews in the world – once they've gathered in Israel. "Just on a personal level, I found [Nasrallah] remarkable," Hanon told Evangelical journalist Jim Fletcher.

Mart Green hired a writer who was smitten by Hassan Nasrallah, the leader of one of the most anti-Semitic organizations on the planet to produce a film about the Arab-Israeli conflict. This is simply irresponsible.

Publicity photo for the 2010 movie *Little Town of Bethlehem*

The film, which CAMERA recently obtained by purchasing it through Mardel's website, was shown in approximately 400 venues, including Christian colleges and churches throughout the United States and Europe. Operating under the assumption that these viewings attracted an average of 50 attendees (a low estimate, to be sure), CAMERA concludes that at least 20,000 viewers saw this movie. This is a conservative estimate of only one part of the movie's viewing audience, for it was also sold through Amazon and, as stated previously, Mardel's website.

It was also used in course materials at colleges and seminaries including Notre Dame, BIOLA University and Palmer Theological Seminary.

To make matters worse it received three filmmaking awards and was given a positive review by *Christianity Today*.

The movie's wide distribution and the plaudits it received are very troubling given the manner in which it mischaracterized the Arab-Israeli conflict and demonized the Jewish state.

The movie, which ostensibly tells the story of the Israeli-Palestinian peace movement through the lives of an Israeli Jew, a Palestinian Christian and a Palestinian Muslim, is filled with misstatements of facts, material omissions and egregious distortions. For example, the movie falsely indicates that Jews were not regarded with hostility by their Arab neighbors during the British Mandate. The periodic massacres of Jews incited by Haj Amin Al Husseini, the Grand Mufti of Jerusalem, prove this to be false.

The movie also tells viewers that unemployment increased during the Oslo Peace Process and that this increase was one of the contributing factors to the growing popularity of the terror organization, Hamas, prior to the Second Intifada.

In fact, unemployment in both the Gaza Strip and the West Bank decreased during Oslo because of increased job opportunities in Israel.

It was Hamas suicide bombings and the security measures they prompted that caused increases in Palestinian unemployment in 1996. Once the bombings stopped, Israel relaxed the security measures, and unemployment continued to drop until the beginning of the Second Intifada when it went back up dramatically.

The movie got it exactly wrong. Palestinian violence caused Palestinian unemployment, not the other way around.

The film also allows a Palestinian commentator to demonize Israeli voters for electing Benjamin Netanyahu as Prime Minister in 1996, asserting that his election proved a majority of the Israelis "did not want peace." The source does not mention, however, the scores of Israelis who were killed in suicide attacks prior to Netanyahu's election. It was these bombings that helped Netanyahu win the election. Any honest documentary would acknowledge the role these attacks played in the 1996 election. Even *Netanyahu at War*, recently broadcast by Frontline, acknowledged this reality. But Mart Green's movie did not.

The use of such re-enactments disqualifies *Little Town of Bethlehem* as a documentary and reveals the movie to be a manipulative piece of straight up propaganda.

I could go on and on. There are simply too many misstatements of fact and omissions for me to document during my time at this podium. I would have to be here for a couple of hours.

And even if I listed every lie told in *Little Town of Bethlehem*, I still wouldn't get at the worst of what is wrong with this movie.

The film uses propagandistic re-enactments to tell a story of Israeli Jews establishing a life for themselves at the expense of innocent Palestinians. These re-enactments downplay Palestinian hostility and violence toward Israel and Jews while exaggerating Palestinian suffering at the hands of the Israelis. Emblematic of this problem is a re-enactment which details the death of Sami Awad's grandfather, Elias, during the 1948 war.

The re-enactment may not be a reliable description of what happened, because the Awad family has told conflicting stories about how Elias died. Sami tells a story of Elias being killed while putting a white flag on top of his home, but Alex Awad says nothing about a white flag in his version of the story which he tells in his family history. Despite the contradictions, Hanon recreates Sami's unreliable version, a highly propagandistic version of what happened, in gruesome detail, on film for perpetuity.

But the fact that the story is not true is almost beside the point. From CAMERA's perspective, the use of such re-enactments disqualifies *Little Town of Bethlehem* as a documentary and reveals the movie to be a manipulative piece of straight up propaganda, especially since there are no reenactments highlighting the impact of Palestinian violence against Israelis.

The film does show brief flashes of historical footage that highlight acts of violence against Israelis, but they are without context. For example, the movie provides a short visual acknowledgment of the massacre of Israeli athletes at the 1972 Olympics in Munich, but this choppy and incoherent segment concludes with a statement from Sami Awad saying that such attacks should not be used to stereotype all Palestinians as terrorists.

Awad's response ignores an important point: The Munich massacre was perpetrated under orders from Yassir Arafat, who gained power as a result of the Oslo Accords. Awad himself could not bring himself to condemn the massacres, but merely asserted that they should not be condoned or praised.

That's not the condemnation a true peacemaker would offer.

This brings me to how the film posits a false equivalence between the Palestinian cause and the American civil rights movement led by Martin Luther King Jr. In the film, Sami Awad tells viewers that "The First Intifada is a lot like the Civil Rights movement in the U.S."

There is simply no comparison between the cause of the PLO, which perpetrated the Munich Massacre, and the Civil Rights movement led by Martin Luther King.

Viewers are shown footage of the protesters being attacked by Bull Connor's police juxtaposed with images of Palestinians fighting with Israeli soldiers as if there was an equivalence between the two.

However, the fight for civil rights was not associated with overt calls for genocide or the destruction of the American republic, but was marked by Martin Luther King's call for African Americans to be accorded their God-given rights described in the U.S. Constitution.

Elsewhere in the movie, Sami Awad equates the demand of African American leaders in the U.S. for equality and freedom with the PLO's demand for recognition. This too, is simply outrageous. The PLO is a conglomeration of terror organizations that have regularly called for Israel's destruction and have promoted the worst sort of Jew-hatred in Palestinian society. There is simply no comparison between the cause of the PLO, which perpetrated the Munich Massacre, and the Civil Rights movement led by Martin Luther King.

Director Jim Hanon dishonestly invokes the image of Martin Luther King, Jr. in his movie, *Little Town of Bethlehem.*

MLK would condemn Palestinian leaders who regularly call for Israel's destruction and promote vicious Jew-hatred but this movie, ostensibly devoted to promoting Dr. King's vision, makes no reference to incitement in Palestinian society.

MLK regularly affirmed Israel's right to exist and need for security, telling the national convention of the Rabbinical Assembly in 1968 that "Peace for Israel means security, and that security must be a reality."

Call for Apology

The movie's bias is so strong that something more than carelessness or ignorance on the part of the film's writer and director, Jim Hanon, is at play. *Little Town of Bethlehem* exhibits a hostile bias against the Jewish state and an undeniable attempt to propagandize against Israel and its supporters in the United States.

People who watch this film and believe what it says will regard Israel as a monstrous nation and those who claim it as their homeland as monsters as well. Given the rising tide of antisemitism – which was a problem well before the release of this movie – Green's decision to produce and distribute this movie was a fundamentally irresponsible act.

While CAMERA has been told by a number of sources that Mart Green no longer supports the message offered by *Little Town of Bethlehem,* he has yet to publicly disavow himself from the video, which can still be purchased on Amazon and is still promoted on Facebook. This is inexcusable.

As we look at what is happening in Europe, where Jews are regularly attacked and in some instances killed because they are Jews, we must remember that virulent anti-Zionism – like what we see in *Little Town of Bethlehem* – helped pave the way for this hostility. Given what's at stake, Mart Green needs to do more than privately admit that there were serious problems with the movie.

He needs to apologize publicly and embark on a campaign to correct the record.

Mart Green has yet to publicly disavow himself from the video, which can still be purchased on Amazon and is still promoted on Facebook.

To be effective, this campaign would require the publication and distribution of a fact sheet that would be sent to all of the consumers who purchased the movie through online venues.

This sheet, which should be sent to officials at the 400 venues where the movie was shown, would include a list of the problems with the movie and the reality as it should have been presented in the film.

The campaign would also include the preparation and distribution of a press release drawing attention to his efforts to correct the record. This release would need to be sent to relevant media outlets, including *Christianity Today*, which gave the movie a positive review.

Conclusion

In conclusion, I want to briefly draw your attention to the sexual assaults on women that took place in Europe over New Year's Eve. These were perpetrated by Muslim radicals who have no respect for the Western values of equality and dignity for women. There are numerous reports of a concerted effort to keep the story of these attacks out of the media.

What do these assaults have to do with anti-Zionism?

The problems that afflicted the Middle East for so long – hostility toward Jews, lack of respect for human rights, hostility toward religious freedom, and contempt for women – are now making their way west through both the Internet and immigration.

In a word, everything. The inability of European elites to respond appropriately to these attacks is the result of the moral and intellectual failure that started with the embrace of anti-Zionism in Europe in the 1970s.

Anti-Zionist activists trained, if you will, their neighbors to turn a blind eye to the anti-Israel incitement, hostility and violence that had been a problem in the Middle East for decades.

As journalists, intellectuals, religious leaders and politicians became de-sensitized to this violence, they lost the ability to identify and speak out against the ideology of Islamism that motivated the attacks on New Year's Eve.

All of this is testimony to the importance of CAMERA's work. In the globalized world in which we live, the problems that afflicted the Middle East for so long – the hostility toward Jews, lack of respect for human rights, hostility toward religious freedom, and contempt for women – are now making their way west through both the Internet and immigration.

Western efforts to formulate a response to these problems have been hindered by the journalists, intellectuals and religious leaders we counted on to inform us about these problems in the Middle East. Instead of telling us the truth about Islamism and Jihadism and its impact on life in the Middle East, Western journalists, human rights activists and religious leaders have encouraged us to view Israel as the problem, rather than the model in the region.

Here is how I think Martin Niemoller would characterize the events of the past few years in Europe:

> First they attacked Israel, but I didn't live in Israel and I thought Israel kind of deserved it, so I didn't speak up.
>
> Then they attacked Jews in Europe, but I was not a Jew, so I did not speak up.
>
> Then they attacked Christians and Yezidis in Iraq and Syria, but I didn't live in Iraq and Syria, so I didn't speak up.
>
> Then they assaulted our wives, sisters and daughters in Europe, but by then I had lost my voice.

In these days in which we live, when the very foundations of our moral and intellectual order are under assault, my message to you is a simple one.

Do not lose your voice.

Be strong.

Let your heart take courage.

And let not your foot be moved.

The *Kairos Palestine Document*, Anti-Israel Boycotts, and How to Combat Them

Malcolm Lowe

Malcolm Lowe holds degrees from Oxford University and is a professor of Philosophy, Christian Backgrounds, and Jewish-Christian Relations at the University of the Holy Land in Jerusalem. He has written extensively on the Kairos Palestine Document, and has been documenting the anti-Zionist leanings of prominent Palestinian Christians such as Mitri Raheb for many years.

The so-called *Kairos Palestine Document* was launched in Bethlehem on December 11, 2009 with the following original signatories:

His Beatitude Patriarch Michel Sabbah, His Eminence Archbishop Atallah Hanna, Bishop Munib Younan, Rev. Dr. Jamal Khader, Rev. Dr. Rafiq Khoury, Rev. Dr. Mitri Raheb, Rev. Dr. Naim Ateek, Rev. Dr. Yohana Katanacho, Rev. Fadi Diab, Dr. Jiries Khoury. Ms. Cedar Duaybis , Ms. Nora Kort, Ms. Lucy Thaljieh , Mr. Nidal Abu El Zuluf, Mr. Yusef Daher , Mr. Rifat Kassis - Coordinator

Content of the Document

Despite the length of the document, each of its nine sections embodies an idea that can easily be summed up in a few words, sometimes by a single paragraph. In Section 1, "The Reality on the Ground," the concept is this:

> Yes, there is Palestinian resistance to the occupation. However, if there were no occupation, there would be no resistance, no fear and no insecurity. This is our understanding of the situation. Therefore, we call on the Israelis to end the occupation. Then they will see a new world in which there is no fear, no threat but rather security, justice and peace.

Quite notably, this summary whitewashes Palestinian terrorism and propagates the lie that terrorism will vanish when the "occupation" is over. Even more notably, "The Reality on the Ground" was written after the withdrawal of all Israeli presence in Gaza, which was followed by increased terror. The fact that Israel has been subjected to continuous attack via missiles and tunnels after turning Gaza over to Palestinian rule refutes the claim that the only reason there are attacks is due to the so-called "occupation."

The key passage of Section 2, "A Word of Faith," is:

> We also declare that the Israeli occupation of Palestinian land is a sin against God and humanity because it deprives the Palestinians of their basic human rights, bestowed by God. It distorts the image of God in the Israeli who has become an occupier just as it distorts this image in the Palestinian living under occupation. We declare that any theology, seemingly based on the Bible or on faith or on history, that legitimizes the occupation, is far from Christian teachings, because it calls for violence and holy war in the name of God Almighty, subordinating God to temporary human interests, and distorting the divine image in the human beings living under both political and theological injustice.

Here they claim that Christian theology that legitimizes Jewish sovereignty, whether "based on the Bible or on faith or on history," is in reality not Christian. Rather, according to their view, God has bestowed the Land of Israel, aka Palestine, not upon the Jewish People, but upon the Palestinians.

This is actually the key concept that underlies all the books of so-called "Palestinian theology" written by Naim Ateek and Mitri Raheb, two of the signers of *Kairos Palestine*. Ateek, a Palestinian Anglican priest and the founder of the Sabeel Ecumenical Liberation Theology Center in Jerusalem, and Raheb, pastor of the Evangelical Lutheran Christmas Church in Bethlehem, have both authored books and articles that reinterpret the Bible and Christian theology in order to promote the Palestinian political narrative.

Here they claim that Christian theology that legitimizes Jewish sovereignty, whether "based on the Bible or on faith or on history," is in reality not Christian.

In particular, Ateek and Raheb both believe that the Palestinians have replaced the Jews as the Chosen People of God. You will hardly find this doctrine stated in as many words; it is rather a conclusion that the readers are encouraged to draw for themselves. The impact of those texts has indeed been, as their authors intended, to convince entire church bodies and congregations that the Palestinians must become the central focus of Christian faith.

Sections 3 and 4 of the *Kairos Palestine Document* are entitled "Hope" and "Love." The former details how the authors seek support for their aims from churches, the international community, Israelis and Jews. "Love" is about how to combat Israel, whether by so-called "resistance," or by calling "on individuals, companies and states to engage in divestment and economic and commercial boycott of everything produced by the occupation."

Rev. Naim Ateek, signer of *Kairos Palestine*

The remaining sections are directed at various named audiences. A "Word to Our Brothers and Sisters" (chiefly Palestinian Christians, section 5) is followed by their "Word to the Churches of the World" (section 6). Here the authors issue a "message of solidarity" with their Christian supporters and a "call to repentance" directed against "fundamentalist theological positions." In other words, good Christians are those who support Palestinian political aims unconditionally, and bad Christians are those who sympathize with Israel.

Rev. Mitri Raheb, pastor of the Evanglical Lutheran Christmas Church in Bethlehem

Next (section 7) comes a "Word to the International Community." It is a call for "the beginning of a system of economic sanctions and boycott to be applied against Israel." Note that it will no longer be merely a "boycott of everything produced by the occupation" (as in section 2) but a boycott of Israel as such.

After an address to "Jewish and Muslim Religious Leaders" (section 8) comes a "Call to our Palestinian People and to the Israelis" (section 9). Here they "appeal to the international community to lend its support towards this union and to respect the will of the Palestinian people as expressed freely." This was a reference to the victory of Hamas in the 2006 election to the Palestinian parliament.

Indeed, there are other statements in the document that suggest that the true agenda of its authors is the replacement of Israel with a unitary state of Palestine.

Hamas, of course, rejects the very existence of Israel. Indeed, there are other statements in the document that suggest that the primary agenda of its authors is the replacement of Israel with a unitary State of Palestine with an Arab majority ensured by the so-called "right of return" of refugees. Just like its endorsement of the Palestinians as the Chosen People of God, this conclusion is stated not in so many words, but is implied repeatedly by less blatant assertions. A second principal aim of the document is the attempt to delegitimize Christian sympathy for Israel and specifically the Bible-based love Evangelical Protestants have for the Jewish People.

Impact of the Document

I pointed out the devious character of the document in the New English Review (April 2010) as did a number of others. I also pointed out that the document's pretensions to speak for all Christians of the Holy Land were spurious, as demonstrated by the identities of the rest of the signatories.

For example, Michel Sabbah was entitled, "Latin Patriarch," although he had already retired from that post. Archbishop Atallah Hanna by no means represented the Greek Orthodox Patriarchate, and reports on the Internet (2007) claimed that he had been disciplined for trying to undermine the Patriarch. As for Bishop Munib Younan, he quickly asked for his name to be withdrawn from the list of authors, so as not to damage his relations with Israel. (Unfortunately for him, reports on numerous websites had already listed him as an author and they can still be read online.) The other signatories are laypeople and low-level clerics who, in spite of the fact that they include those with a long record of agitation against Israel, cannot be considered spokespersons for all Christians in the Holy Land.

Several relevant church bodies issued critical comments and a number of theologians ridiculed its theological pretensions.

Rev. Michel Sabbah, former Latin Patriarch

Archbishop Atallah Hanna

For these reasons, among others, the impact of the document has been slow and limited. Although the authors include Catholics, its uptake in the Roman Catholic Church was small, apart from the militant "peacemakers" of Pax Christi. The leadership of a few Protestant churches love it, such as the United Church of Christ, the Church of Sweden, the British Methodists and the Church of Scotland. In Germany, initial confusion was caused by the mention of Bishop Younan, and after he withdrew his name, several relevant church bodies issued critical comments and a number of theologians ridiculed its theological pretensions.

The biggest propagator of *Kairos Palestine* has been the Secretariat of the World Council of Churches (WCC). Indeed, the document was largely a scheme of the Secretariat from the beginning, as Rifat Kassis, the coordinator of *Kairos Palestine,* was a veteran WCC employee and Yusef Daher, its current main propagator, does so as a WCC employee.

Bishop Munib Younan

The Heads of Churches in Jerusalem were evidently alarmed by the attempt of the signatories of the document to claim to represent all local Christians. Four days later, they published a brief response:

> We, the Patriarchs and Heads of Churches in Jerusalem, hear the cry of hope that our children have launched in these difficult times that we still experience in this Holy Land. We support them and stand by them in their faith, their hope, their love and their vision for the future. We also support the call to all our faithful as well as to the Israeli and Palestinian Leaders, to the International Community and to the World Churches, in order to accelerate the achievement of justice, peace and reconciliation in this Holy Land. We ask God to bless all our children by giving them more power in order to contribute effectively in establishing and developing their community, while making it a community of love, trust, justice and peace.

The WCC seized upon this statement to claim that the Heads of Churches had endorsed the document. Subsequently, both the WCC and the *Kairos Palestine* website prefixed the text of the document with this statement, as if the document had been issued by the Heads of Churches themselves.

However, the statement of the Heads of Churches, taken by itself, avoids all the inflammatory language and theological nonsense of the document. Indeed, the statement hints that its authors should concentrate on building up the local Christian communities rather than engage in political agitation. I exposed the deception of combining the statement with the document in my article of April 2010, and later critics took up this issue as well. In particular, the whole section entitled "Controversy about prefatory statement" in the Wikipedia entry on *Kairos Palestine* consists of a summary from my article.

The Heads of Churches in Jerusalem were evidently alarmed by the attempt of the signatories of the document to claim to represent all local Christians.

Currently, perhaps in reaction to criticism, the English version of the document on the *Kairos Palestine* website lacks both the statement of the Heads of Churches and a list of authors. But the Dutch version, for instance, still has both and still includes Bishop Younan as an author.

How to Combat Anti-Israel Boycotts

Last year (July 2015), on the website of the Gatestone Institute, I published an article entitled "Combating Anti-Israel Boycotts: The Underused Strategies." The strategies that I classified and described, however, have applications to other kinds of anti-Israel activity, not just to boycotts. So it will be useful to outline those strategies and see how they can be applied to the *Kairos Palestine* phenomenon, including my own approach in the New English Review. By the way, it was thanks to Dexter Van Zile that the article could appear there.

There are at least two basic kinds of strategy. On the one hand, there are strategies that defend Israel's good name. For example, denouncing lies and half-truths or complaining that criticism is directed exclusively at Israel and ignores the horrible misdeeds perpetrated by governments of other countries. In other words: loudly complaining that "It's not fair!"

Most organizations combating anti-Israel activity primarily use these strategies, including CAMERA. It works for CAMERA, because much of CAMERA's activity is directed toward major news media, which are professionally committed to fairness. It also works when NGO Monitor tackles government funding for anti-Israel NGOs, since those governments must respect relevant legislation. Mostly, however, one cries "It's not fair!" in vain, because anti-Israel activists have no interest whatsoever in being fair. The main essential task performed by these strategies is to prevent the subversion of Israel's friends or of the non-committed.

There are at least two basic kinds of strategy. On the one hand, there are strategies that defend Israel's good name.

On the other hand, there are offensive strategies that target the boycotters. The principal behind these strategies is: "This is going to hurt you more than us." Following are four ways to work against those who fight against Israel using methods that will hurt the boycotters.

Use Lawfare

It is a mistake made by NGO Monitor and others to define "lawfare" as "abuse of the law to attack Israel." The correct definition, following the acknowledged expert Charles Dunlap (2001) is: "the use of law as a weapon of war." Israel's friends can use the law just as its enemies abuse it. The Israeli organization Shurat HaDin uses it very effectively. Recent judgments given in France, the UK and Spain show that BDS activity is vulnerable.

Institute Counter-Boycotts

Having identified the boycotters, institute boycotts of them. Most conveniently, boycotters often publish long lists of their supporters, facilitating their pursuit. Consult Canary Mission, which has compiled profiles of many campus enemies of Israel.

Show How Anti-Israel Activity is Self-Hurting

Point out how anti-Israel activity may end up hurting only the institution that does it. For instance, when a church starts to get involved with "Palestine," it imports all the hatreds of the Palestinian problem into the hearts of its parishes, making its members start fighting among themselves, as some vehemently support "Palestine" while others defend Israel. Wax eloquent over how Israel goes from strength to strength, how the Palestinians benefit not a whit from the church's attack on Israel, while only the church itself suffers. Dexter Van Zile wrote a brilliant article about this in April 2010, titled "A Shipwreck of Their Faith" (New English Review). But it is not enough to write once: one must gloat about it endlessly until it becomes a commonplace that causes misery for those who seek to harm Israel, whenever they try to do it.

Point out how anti-Israel activity may end up hurting only the institution that does it.

Delegitimize Israel Haters

Seize on anything that will undermine respect for haters of Israel. If they are academics, deride those who come from minor institutions and pick holes in their research. In churches, point out agitators who are merely petty bureaucrats with minimal theological training. An example of a successful delegitimization of an Israel hater is that of Samuel Kobia, who gave up his post as General Secretary of the World Council of Churches (WCC) after doubts arose about the validity of the Ph.D. in his Curriculum Vitae.

Application of the Case of *Kairos Palestine* to Anti-Israel Boycotts

The *Kairos Palestine Document* has been significantly discredited by a combination of the "It's not fair!" arguments about the content, and the delegitimization of its authors. It is also compromised by the fact that the WCC cooked up this scheme while the discredited Kobia served as General Secretary from 2004-2009.

It has become evident that churches that try to promote *Kairos Palestine* primarily hurt themselves, because they can be boycotted. Churches that have based their own documents upon it can be exposed and boycotted until they withdraw those documents. For example, *Kairos*-inspired documents adopted by the British Methodists and the Church of Scotland are riddled with deceptions and theological nonsense. In light of this exposure, these churches should to be shunned until they officially withdraw those documents.

Unfortunately, nobody – including Jewish communities – has yet taken up these weapons. But just as the *Kairos Palestine Document* has been discredited by a combination of methods, anti-Israel boycotts can be successfully combated by using offensive strategies that target the boycotters.

Antidotes for the Threat to Evangelical Support for Israel

Countering the Threats to Evangelical Support of Israel

Laurie Cardoza-Moore, Th.M.

Dr. Laurie Cardoza-Moore has devoted her life to educating Christians about their Biblical responsibility to stand with their Jewish brethren and the State of Israel. In 2005, she became the founder and president of Proclaiming Justice to The Nations, an organization that utilizes the powerful medium of documentary films to educate Christians and facilitate dialogue between the Christian and Jewish communities.

Anti-Semitism is rearing its ugly head again and Christians must understand how dangerous this is, not only for the Jews, but for all of Western civilization. We expect anti-Semitism and anti-Zionism from the mainline denominations, but we don't expect it from Evangelicals because, after all, Evangelicals usually read the Bible and know what it says about Israel and the Jewish people. However, Evangelical support for Israel can no longer be taken for granted.

In 1938, Hitler gave everyone in Germany a radio, and then he began his diatribes. Harry Truman understood the impact of the media and he believed that if he could just broadcast the simple unvarnished truth on Radio Free Europe, he could educate the masses. He was successful.

This is why the work that CAMERA and Proclaiming Justice to the Nations are doing in the media, fighting these issues in the media, is critically important. If we don't spread this message globally, if we don't stand up, if Jews and Christians do not unite together this time, we are going to be in trouble once again.

As we look around the globe, we are confounded by events in the Middle East, in Europe, and even now in the United States. We live in a challenging and sober time in human history. Many of us believe we're coming to the climax of that history.

If we look closely, we see a biblical warning that in the latter days, even the elect will be deceived. We have been warned that we must keep our doctrine sound and pure. As II Timothy 3:1 says, "In the last days difficult times will come. And many will turn away their ears from the truth, and will turn aside to myths."

Jesus warned his disciples of the deception in the last days, in Matthew 24, when he said, "For false Christs and false prophets will arise and will show great signs and wonders, as to mislead, if possible, even the elect."

If we don't stand up, if Jews and Christians do not unite together this time, we are going to be in trouble once again.

Is this happening today in the Evangelical Church? I would say that it is, and the trend is alarming, to say the least.

In the scriptures, God made an everlasting covenant with the nation of Israel and the Jewish people. That covenant was confirmed in the Torah, in the Prophets, and in the New Testament writings. For Christians, the first five books of the Old Testament – the Torah – are the plumb line for our faith. The Prophets and the New Testament writings attest to what the

Torah says about the covenant between God and Israel. If our understanding does not line up with what is written, then we are following false doctrines and traditions.

The Bible is a book written to Israel, for Israel and about Israel. And as Paul stated in Ephesians, Chapter 2, Gentiles come into the Commonwealth of Israel through faith in Yeshua. It is extremely important that we understand this, because this will determine how we perceive Israel and the Jewish people.

The purpose of this monograph is to discuss the threats and challenges to Evangelical Christian support for Israel, and the relationship between Evangelicals and the Jewish people. I am going to focus on the history of this support, the threats to Jewish-Christian relations, and how we can counter current threats to both the support and our relationship.

History of Jewish-Christian Relations

We are seeing a move of God that is unprecedented in history. Christians and Jews are uniting together in a growing relationship that the prophet Isaiah foretold. But it hasn't always been this way. To understand the significance of what is happening today, we must look at our anti-Semitic past and come to terms with it.

Christian anti-Semitism can be traced back to the great divide between the two faiths. It became official policy during the reign of the Roman Emperor, Constantine the Great (306-337 CE). Constantine's sword sliced away all remnants of the Hebrew roots of Christianity and led to the birth of the Catholic Church. Church leaders formulated the false charge of deicide against the Jews, and the libel that Jews are "Christ killers" still haunts our world today.

During the Middle Ages in Europe there was widespread, full-scale persecution that included blood libels, expulsions, forced conversions and massacres. Jews were banned from owning land and from pursuing a number of professions. Persecution by the Church in Spain and Portugal led to the infamous and brutal Inquisition.

In 1516, the Republic of Venice decreed that Jews would only be allowed to reside in a walled-in area of town called the ghetto. This requirement soon spread across Europe. Jews became scapegoats, and in Eastern Europe and Russia, they faced constant pogroms and persecution. The tsar's chief adviser reportedly said that one-third of Russia's Jews were expected to emigrate, one-third to accept baptism, and one-third to starve.

Constantine's sword sliced away all remnants of the Hebrew roots of Christianity.

The reformation led by Martin Luther began in earnest in the sixteenth century. Luther at first wrote kindly about the Jews, hoping they would come to faith in Christ as a result. However, when they refused to convert, Luther's writings became extremely anti-Semitic. These writings were later used by the Nazis to justify their actions against the Jews. Thus, even Hitler's final solution had some basis in Christian anti-Semitism.

Martin Luther

The Nobel Prize writer and Holocaust survivor, Elie Wiesel, famously said that there were two types of people before the Second World War – those who killed Jews and those who did nothing. We look back and wonder how a highly civilized and educated Christian nation could turn its back on the genocide of the Jews. In fact how could most of the world do likewise? Is it any wonder that many Jewish people are skeptical of Christians who offer them support?

History of Evangelical Support for Israel

In spite of this past, there have been Christians throughout history who stood against the hate and helped protect and save Jews. There was a root of Christian love and acceptance of the Jewish people. From such love grew the seedling of a rebirth of Israel.

In nineteenth century England, there were many advocates in favor of a Jewish state in their ancient homeland.

Lord Arthur Balfour

We often think that the first Christian to push for the establishment of the Jewish state was Lord Balfour. In 1917, as British Foreign Secretary, Lord Balfour wrote his landmark declaration to establish a homeland for the Jews in Palestine. But even before Balfour, a deep-seated philosophical and religious movement had taken root in British soil. That movement was called Christian Zionism.

Lord Shaftesbury

In nineteenth century England, there were many advocates in favor of a Jewish state in their ancient homeland. The most notable of these were: John Nelson Darby, Lord Palmerston, Lord Manchester, Sir George Gawler, Lord Lindsay, and Lord Shaftesbury.

Lord Shaftesbury was the most active restoration lobbyist. He stated that he "never had a shadow of a doubt that the Jews were to return to their own land." It was his daily prayer, his daily hope. "Oh pray for the peace of Jerusalem!" were the words engraved on the ring he always wore on his right hand.

So clearly, Christian support for Israel is not just a modern-day phenomenon. It is rooted in people who understood that the Bible was about ISRAEL, not the church.

Yes, Christians played a major role in the establishment of Israel. They became instruments in fulfilling the Word spoken through the Prophet Isaiah (Isaish 66:7-9).

> Before she was in labor, she gave birth; Or shall a nation be born at once?
> For as soon as Zion was in labor, She gave birth to her children.
> "Shall I bring to the time of birth, and not cause delivery?" says the LORD.
> "Shall I who cause delivery shut up the womb?" says your God."

However, even though the relationship between Christians, Jews and Israel has blossomed in recent history, the seed of the oldest hatred never died.

Threats to This Relationship: The New Anti-Semitism

With the birth of Israel we've seen the rise of a new anti-Semitism – a hatred of Zionism, Israel and the Jewish people all wrapped together. I suppose this is not a surprise from the secular world, but should we expect it from Christians as well, and for that matter, even from Evangelical Christians who claim to believe the Bible?

It is noteworthy that, in spite of the claim the conference is held for the purpose of promoting peace, there are no representatives from Israel among the speakers or attendees.

Indeed, history and hatred do repeat themselves. Currently, false doctrine is being taught, and large numbers of people are deceived into believing that Israel must give up the right to her God-given land. It is really frightening to see that more and more Christians and denominations are falling headlong into this treacherous heresy.

Proponents of this Christian version of anti-Zionism include respected evangelical leaders such as Bill & Lynne Hybels. The Hybels are the founders of Willow Creek Church, which is one of the most influential evangelical churches in the U.S. This church has almost 25,000 congregants in the Chicago area, and it is the head of an international organization that influences more than 80,000 leaders from over 13,000 congregations worldwide.

Lynne Hybels is one of the biggest proponents of the Christ at the Checkpoint conferences, which propagate dangerous anti-Israel heresy on a very large scale. The host of this anti-Semitic conference, held every two years in Bethlehem, is Bethlehem Bible College, an influential promoter of the same anti-Zionist false narrative Willow Creek Church espouses.

Attendees at Christ at the Checkpoint include Christian pastors, Christian students, Christian publishers, Christian authors, Christian Jews, and Christian reporters. In addition to the Christian attendees, an Islamic spokesman for the Palestinian Authority kicks off the conference – right after everyone stands to sing the Palestinian National Anthem. It is noteworthy that, in spite of the claim that the conference is held for the purpose of promoting peace, there are no representatives from Israel among the speakers or attendees.

With the birth of Israel we've seen the rise of a new anti-Semitism — a hatred of Zionism, Israel and the Jewish people all wrapped together.

Another proponent of Christian anti-Zionism is World Vision, a highly respected and extremely influential organization in the Evangelical Christian world. World Vision's Middle East program in Jerusalem, Gaza and the West Bank has a staff of 140 people and a $16 million dollar budget. Tom Getman, a former activist with World Vision, recently acknowledged his close affiliation with leaders of the terrorist organization, Hezbollah.

And finally, a discussion of Christians who help to propagate Christian anti-Zionism would not be complete without mentioning Mart Green, heir to the Hobby Lobby retail chain. In 2010, he financed and produced *Little Town of Bethlehem*, a documentary that erroneously portrays Palestinians as peace loving people trying to survive a cruel Israeli government that is oppressing Arab Christians and Muslims.

All of these Christian leaders and organizations use spurious narratives in their efforts to discourage Evangelical support for Israel. For example, they claim that because Jesus was oppressed by the Romans, he had more in common with the oppressed Palestinians than current-day Jews. This is because, according to their story, the Jews are occupying Palestinian land and have no right to this land since they forfeited their covenant as a result of their rejection of Jesus.

A relatively new front in the war against Israel, and against those who support Israel, is an insidious new form of anti-Semitism cloaked in a deceptive narrative that claims to be about "human rights" for Palestinians. It promotes the smear that Israel is an apartheid country, an oppressor, an occupier.

This campaign is known as BDS, or the boycott, divestment and sanctions movement.
BDS groups call on the international community "to impose broad boycotts and implement divestment initiatives against Israel similar to those applied to South Africa in the apartheid era." Proponents of BDS also call for pressure on governments "to impose embargoes and sanctions against Israel."

This movement is now fueling the violent Israel Apartheid demonstrations we're seeing on college campuses in the U.S. today. And BDS groups and their supporters are pouring millions of dollars and organizational assets into influencing millennial Christians so that the future of the relationship between Evangelicals and Israel will be changed in favor of the Palestinian cause.

How Can We Counter Threats Such as BDS?

There are two crucial questions that need to be asked. The first one is: how can we counter new and dangerous threats to evangelical support of Israel such as BDS?

Disinformation is the bread and butter of BDS, and it is what BDS promoters rely on to push their agenda of anti-Semitism, anti-Zionism, and their ultimate goal, which is the elimination of the State of Israel.

One very important way is through information. This is because disinformation is the fuel that drives BDS, and includes lies that are spread through the media, anti-Semitic groups and even school textbooks. Disinformation is the bread and butter of BDS, and it is what BDS promoters rely on to push their agenda of anti-Semitism, anti-Zionism, and their ultimate goal, which is the elimination of the State of Israel.

Proclaiming Justice to the Nations is on the front lines in the war to destroy the BDS movement, and is combating BDS in a three-prong fashion. We have started a K-12 textbook initiative to correct the lies taught to our children. We are sponsoring legislation that fights BDS on college campuses and halts illegal boycotts and divestments. And we are producing media aimed at the millennial generation.

In May of 2015, we began production of a feature-length documentary that will target millennial Christians and will expose the lies and anti-Semitism of the BDS movement. This film will be made in a style called "docutainment," and will examine the false and ridiculous claims against Israel using satire and humor.
We know that like a great story, satire and humor can work as a Trojan horse and penetrate intellectual walls. Finding ways to work wit into a decidedly unpleasant subject matter can seriously challenge someone's view and cause them to reexamine what they believed to be the truth. Brad Stine, a popular college comedian and political commentator, is the host in this cinematic quest for truth.

The plan for distribution includes a limited theatrical release that targets a millennial audience with screenings on college campuses and theatrical showings in college towns. This work is critical because if this audience is not reached with the truth about the BDS movement, the future of America's support for Israel could fade or evaporate completely.

How Do We Preserve the Relationship?

The second question is: what can we do to preserve and nurture the relationship between Christians, Jews and Israel, for the sake of Israel and for the sake of the Jewish people? More specifically, what is our responsibility as Christians to Israel and the Jewish people?

God told the prophet Obadiah that in the last days, he would wipe out the descendants of Edom because they stood by and did nothing while their brother Jacob (Israel) was held in captivity. So, what do we need to do differently this time as we witness the rise of the "new" anti-Semitism?

What is our responsibility as Christians to Israel and the Jewish people?

First, we must read and understand Scripture with an understanding of its Hebraic roots, and not according to false doctrines and traditions of men.

Second, we must make a difference in our community. Making a difference starts with teaching our children the truth, and continues with educating others to enable them to stand against the anti-Semitism and replacement theology that is still pervasive in many segments of the Christian Church.

Third, contact your Congressmen and Senators when Israel's back is against the wall. And in election years, be sure you are registered to vote, and then vote!

And finally, get involved with Proclaiming Justice to the Nations and CAMERA to help us mobilize the global Christian community on behalf of our Jewish brethren and Israel.

The Case for Israel

Shadi Khalloul

Shadi Khalloul is Chairman of the Israeli Aramaic Christian Association, and acts as a spokesperson for the Christian Israel Defense Forces (IDF) Forum. He served as a lieutenant in a paratrooper division of the IDF, and is now a captain in the reserves. He is a strong advocate of close relationships between Christian and Jews, and what he has to say about life in Israel offers a powerful antidote to Christian anti-Zionist propaganda.

I am an Israeli Aramean Christian. Arameans have a very long presence and history in Israel and the surrounding region.

In ancient times, when the first fruit offerings were brought to the Temple, the Jews recited the following verse from Deuteronomy 26:5: "Arami oved avi," which means, "My father was a wandering Aramean." Jesus himself must have surely spoken these words when he visited the Temple. The Bible identifies Jacob as an Aramean before God gave him the name Israel and made him the father of a holy nation, his chosen people.

Flag of the Syriac-Aramaic People

God made an everlasting covenant with Abraham, Isaac and Jacob saying: "I will make of you a great nation, and I will bless you; I will make your name great, and you will be a blessing. I will bless those who bless you, and whoever curses you I will curse; and all peoples on earth will be blessed through you." (Gen. 12:2-3) God promised to preserve the Jewish people for all times and to give them the land of Israel forever.

As a result, this holy land is forever connected to the Jewish people through the oath God swore to the fathers and the unconditional promises he made to the people of Israel. The Bible is full of evidence of this truth. From Genesis to the prophets and throughout the New Testament, it is evident that Israel and the Jewish people have a central role in God's salvation plan. The regathering of the Jews from all the nations in the world to the land of Israel is God's work and is the fulfillment of the prophesies in the Bible. Israel was and still is "bavat eino," the apple of God's eye. (Zech. 2:12)

We have many reasons to bless Israel as a result of our deep theological, historical, and ethnic connections to the Jewish people.

Today, we Arameans are a Christian minority living as citizens of Israel. We support Israel and love the Jewish people, to which we have close ethnic and religious ties. Some of us even call our sons "Israel," demonstrating our passion and connection to God's chosen people. We have the same roots and are from one family. Many ancient Jewish traditions survived in our Aramean (Syriac) churches, even traditions from the Jewish Temple. We speak Aramaic, the language of the Jews at the time of Jesus. We have many reasons to bless Israel as a result of our deep theological, historical, and ethnic connections to the Jewish people.

With this as context, I would like to address the following questions: How does Israel treat

Christians in particular and non-Jews in general? And, what are Israel's moral norms in its treatment of others?

Israel's Treatment of Christians in Particular

Israel is a democratic country that grants full civil rights, freedom and liberty to all its citizens, regardless of whether they are Jews or non-Jews. The Jewish State not only grants minorities full rights, but strengthens minority communities through a variety of state-sponsored programs. To me, as an Aramean Christian citizen born in the State, Israel has proven itself as an absolutely moral and fair country.

When I was 19-years-old, I served as a paratrooper lieutenant in the IDF. The IDF trusted me, a non-Jewish Aramean Christian, and my loyalty as an Israeli citizen. They placed 100 young Jewish soldiers straight out of high school under my supervision, putting their lives in my hands. I led them in the field, was responsible for their needs and was like a father to them during their three years of military service. There are 1500 Christian soldiers who serve in the IDF today and receive the same treatment from young Jewish officers.

To me, as an Aramean Christian citizen born in the State, Israel has proven itself as an absolutely moral and fair country.

Prime Minister Benjamin Netanyahu

Since my service in the IDF, I have held many different positions and have benefited from the same freedom to explore job opportunities as any other Israeli citizen looking for a successful career.

As Prime Minister Netanyahu has stated:

> Israel's minorities, including over one million citizens who are Arabs, always have full civil rights. Israel's government will never tolerate discrimination against women. Israel's Christian population will always be free to practice their faith. This is the only place in the Middle East where Christians are fully free to practice their faith. They don't have to fear; they don't have to flee. In a time where Christians are under siege in so many places, in so many lands in the Middle East, I'm proud that in Israel, Christians are free to practice their faith and that there's a thriving Christian community in Israel.

I can assure you these words are true. Christians and other minorities in Israel do prosper and grow, whereas in other countries in the Middle East they suffer greatly.

The Aramean Christian Experience in Israel

Last year, in a historic move, the State of Israel recognized us Arameans as a distinct ethnic and religious nationality. This means that Israel accepts the existence of a Christian people within its borders, acknowledges our historic roots and gives us the legal right to strengthen and develop our community. No other country in the world has ever done this before.

Pro-Palestinian opponents of self-determination for Christian Arameans, followed by some international media, accused Israel of weakening the Palestinian identity by separating Christian Arabs from Muslim Arabs. But the actions of the State of Israel reflect its democratic moral values, and were done in response to the request of the Aramean community, which does not consider itself Arab. Therefore, it is unjust and prejudicial to condemn Israel for her democratic actions.

Those who criticize Israel are not driven by concern for minorities or justice, but by hatred of the Jewish state.

Contrast the status of Arameans who live in Israel with the status of those who live in Turkey. For almost one hundred years, Arameans in Turkey have been attempting to gain the legal status and minority rights guaranteed by the Lausanne Treaty of 1923. However, they have still not received the status granted by this internationally recognized treaty.

How much blame has Turkey received from the international community and from the media for refusing to grant rights that are guaranteed under an internationally recognized treaty? The answer is none! Turkey has not been condemned for withholding rights that were granted over ninety years ago.

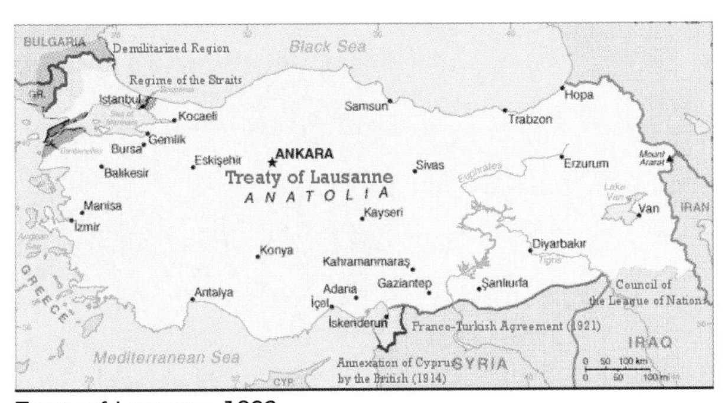

Treaty of Lausanne, 1923

As a result, there are almost no Arameans left in Turkey as of today, although historically it was one of the most populated homelands of our people. While the Aramean population in Turkey continues to dwindle, the number of Christians in Israel is higher now than before the establishment of the Jewish State. This reality is a direct result of Israel's favorable treatment of Christians.

The disparagement of Israel for granting Christians minority rights, and the absence of condemnation for Turkey's denial of those same rights, demonstrates that the international community and the media demonize Israel no matter how just and moral her actions. It reflects a double standard that is neither fair nor moral, and does not tell the truth. What it demonstrates is that those who criticize Israel are not driven by concern for minorities or justice, but by hatred for the Jewish State.

Israel's Treatment of Non-Jews in General

Israel's Declaration of Independence guarantees "full social and political equality of all its citizens without distinction of race, creed and sex." Approximately 24 percent of Israel's population is not Jewish, and is comprised primarily of Arabic-speaking minorities. But from the very beginning, Israel guaranteed its non-Jewish citizens all the rights and privileges of Israeli citizenship, and when the first elections to the Knesset were held in 1949, Israeli Arabs were given the right to vote and to be elected.

The granting of full civil and political rights to non-Jewish minorities means that members of these minorities are free to be active in Israeli social, political and civic life. As a result, they enjoy representation in Israel's Parliament, Foreign Service and judicial system. In addition, we

Christians are joining the Israeli Defense Forces in increased numbers every year. The State of Israel welcomes our participation and integration into all aspects of its society.

Israel has always wanted friends, not enemies. We see this from the words of David Ben Gurion, the first Prime Minister of Israel. In 1947, just before the founding of the State, he said:

> If the Arab citizen will feel at home in our state...if the state will help them in a truthful and dedicated way to reach the economic, social, and cultural level of the Jewish community, then Arab distrust will accordingly subside and a bridge will be built to a Semitic, Jewish-Arab alliance.

Imagine any Muslim State saying this to its non-Muslim citizens. While Islam demands the extermination of Jews and the Jewish State, Israel wants to help its Arab citizens achieve everything its Jewish citizens enjoy.

From the very beginning, Israel guaranteed its non-Jewish citizens all the rights and privileges of Israeli citizenship.

Ben Gurion's inclusion of minorities didn't stop with Arabs within the State, but extended to Christians in the region as well. In 1947, he signed a written agreement with the Maronite Patriarch in Lebanon to establish two national homelands that would provide shelter and protection to persecuted minorities in Middle East – a Christian homeland in Lebanon and a Jewish homeland in Israel.

David Ben-Gurion, First Prime Minister of Israel

Israeli leaders have always been sensitive to the vulnerability and plight of Christians in the entire region. In 1954, Ben Gurion again supported the idea of creating a Christian state in Lebanon as a safe haven for the persecuted Christians of the Middle East.

The State of Israel is doing everything it can to integrate its non-Jewish citizens. Today, many organizations in Israel are trying to promote coexistence among Jews, Arabs, and other minorities, like the Arameans. Government institutions support these organizations, and give national recognition to programs such as our Aramaic Christian Association.

Some Arab Members of Israel's Parliament side with enemies of the country with full impunity.

Through its support of minority culture, and programs for socio-economic well being, the Jewish State shows its acceptance of, and respect for, minorities. This reality stands in stark contrast to the situation in Iran or any other Muslim state, which do not have any program to benefit Christians and other minorities, and where Christians are being persecuted and killed.

As a result of Israel's treatment of non-Jews, the numbers of Christians and Palestinian Arabs have increased significantly since the establishment of the Jewish State. There are currently about 160,000 Christians living in Israel. According to a recent census by Haifa University, "84 percent of Israeli Christians want to integrate into Israeli Jewish society and 74 percent have no problem serving in military or civil service."

Arab citizens of Israel now number more than 1.5 million. They have full rights as citizens and serve in the Knesset. They have more freedom of speech and religion than do citizens of any Arab country in the Middle East. Using this freedom, some Arab Members of Israel's Parliament side with enemies of the country with full impunity. They are free to side with terrorists and are protected by law as they do so.

But even while Israel is working to help preserve the culture of those who want to wipe out the Jewish State, it is falsely accused of ethnic cleansing in the media and in the court of world opinion.

Haneen Zoabi is an Arab member of the Knesset who engages in anti-Israel activism.

Contrast this to Jordanian King Hussein's massacre of thousands of Palestinians for protesting against him in 1970, in what is now known as Black September. Or consider the fact that the Hamas terrorist regime in Gaza slaughtered almost a thousand Palestinian members of Fatah in order to take over the government in Gaza.

Not only have Israeli Arabs kept silent about these atrocities and those committed by other governments, but some of their leaders actually agitate against the one government that allows them the freedom to do just that.

Despite their opposition to the existence of the State, Israel provides support to Arabs for the preservation of their cultural heritage, language and religion (Islam). For example, they have a representative in the Israeli Ministry of Education who is responsible for promoting the language, religion, self-identity and historic roots of the Arabs in the country. In addition, the State develops programs, together with representatives from the Palestinian Arab community, to teach Arabic and Islamic history.

But even while Israel is working to help preserve the culture of those who want to wipe out the Jewish State, it is falsely accused of ethnic cleansing in the media and in the court of world opinion. I do not know of any other country that, while in a constant battle to survive attempts to eradicate it, would continue to treat its enemies in such a moral and tolerant way.

The Use of Christians as Pawns in the War Against Israel

Because Israel provides protection for its minorities, a growing number of Israeli Christians have been calling on their fellow Christians to fully integrate into Israeli society. At the same time, many of us are speaking out against the cynical use of local Christians as pawns in the Palestinian battle against Israel, and in other Arab efforts to destroy Israel as a democratic Jewish State.

Like the majority of Israeli Christians, I feel that many Church leaders are betraying the Christian message and ignoring the rights of fellow Christians in the Holy Land in favor of supporting Islamic propaganda against our country, Israel.

The logo for the 2016 Christ at the Checkpoint Conference

It is quite alarming, therefore, for us as Israeli Christians to see fellow Christians join forces with those who routinely abuse and kill our people in order to falsely accuse Israel, the only country in the region where Christians are actually protected.

It makes me quite angry to see Christian leaders participating in anti-Israel political conferences such as the Christ at the Checkpoint, and I am ashamed of the duplicity of these leaders. In Israel, these Christians enjoy full rights and freedom, including the freedom to publicly slander the State without fear. By contrast, were they to publicly criticize the Palestinian Authority, they and their families would be attacked, imprisoned, tortured and/or killed.

The reality is that there is no comparison between life for Christians in Israel and life for Christians elsewhere in the Middle East. Instead of living in freedom under the protection of the Jewish State, Christians elsewhere in the region are faced with the choice of fleeing, converting to Islam by force, or losing their lives. It is quite alarming, therefore, for us as Israeli Christians to see fellow Christians join forces with those who routinely abuse and kill our people in order to falsely accuse Israel, the only country in the region where Christians are actually protected.

The world needs to know these facts and understand that the people who cynically use the false analogy of Christ at the Checkpoint do not represent the real Christian voice in this region, or anywhere else in the world. We all long for peace in the Holy Land, but it must not be a peace based on lies, as that will only lead to trouble for local Christians. True peace can only come by supporting the democratic State of Israel that protects the rights and freedoms of all minorities.

The Moral Behavior of Minorities in Israel

I have said a lot about Israel's moral norms in its treatment of its minority citizens. So it is only fair to ask: How do those minorities view and treat Israel and its Jewish majority?

The consistent and continued calls for jihad by Palestinian leaders, including Mahmoud Abbas of the Palestinian Authority, inspires and rewards extreme violence against Jews and the State of Israel.

Some minorities, like my own community of Aramean Christians, are loyal citizens who want to support and protect the State of Israel so that it can flourish. Israel is our homeland and the Jews are our brothers. Therefore, we believe we have a duty as citizens to share the same responsibilities as our Jewish fellow citizens. That is why we join the Defense Forces and/or volunteer for the civil services. We do not just want to demand our rights; we want to give something back.

This is not the case when it comes to Arabs who identify as Palestinians, living in the territories and within pre-1967 Israel. Instead of recognizing that their quality of life is much better than that of their brethren in Arab countries, many Palestinian Arabs share the same hatred and genocidal intent toward Jews that is found in Arab society throughout the region.

The Grand Mufti of Jerusalem asked Adolf Hitler for help in exterminating the Jews.

This ideology is not new and has nothing to do with the establishment of the State of Israel because its the establishment of the State of Israel because its roots lie in Islamic theology, which is thirteen hundred-years-old. Even before the establishment of the State, Arabs carried out intifadas against the Jews for the purpose of cleansing the land of Jews. And even in the midst of Germany's Final Solution, the Grand Mufti of Jerusalem met with Adolf Hitler to ask for his assistance in exterminating the Jews in Palestine.

The call for the genocide of Jews by Palestinian Arabs is a serious matter. It is the utmost expression of hate and immorality, and it not only represents a serious threat to the Jewish State, but to all its citizens, including the Christian minority. The consistent and continued calls for jihad by Palestinian leaders, including Mahmoud Abbas of the Palestinian Authority, inspires and rewards extreme violence against Jews and the State of Israel, and has prompted the killing of thousands of innocent civilians in brutal attacks.

The remains of a bombed bus in Jerusalem

When a bus filled with Jewish civilians is blown up by Palestinian terrorists, or suicide bombers detonate themselves in crowded public places such as restaurants and malls, or innocent people are knifed to death as they walk down the street, many Palestinian civilians celebrate by dancing in the streets and distributing candies. The murderers are honored as martyrs, children are named for them, streets and public squares are named after them, and their families receive pensions from the Palestinian Authority.

Indeed, the principal Palestinian Authority religious leader, Grand Mufti Muhammad Hussein, teaches that the killing of Jews by Muslims is a worthy religious goal. At an event celebrating the 47th anniversary of the founding of Fatah in 2012, he cited the Hadith (Islamic tradition attributed to Muhammad), which states:

> The Hour [of Resurrection] will not come until you fight the Jews. The Jew will hide behind stones or trees. Then the stones or trees will call: "Oh Muslim, servant of Allah, there is a Jew behind me, come and kill him."

Unfortunately, this exemplifies the prevailing belief and actions advocated by the civil and religious leadership of the Palestinian Authority. This position is immoral, to say the least, and demonstrates that hatred of Israel and the Jews has nothing to do with how the State treats Arabs, but how Muslim Arabs see Jews as a result of their theology and ideology.

In spite of this reality, and while the world continues to demonize the Jewish State, Israel continues to protect the civil and religious rights of all minorities – even those who are intent on its destruction.

Conclusion

Israel wants peace with its neighbors and with its enemies. It has proven since its establishment in 1948 that it wants to live in peace and harmony with its Arab neighbors. It is not logical or reasonable to think that a nation chooses to live in a constant state of war. Just as every nation on earth wants peace and prosperity, so too does Israel. But how can there be peace when Israel and her citizens are constantly attacked?

Gulda Meir, former Prime Minister of Israel

In 1957, Golda Meir said, "Peace will come to the Middle East when the Arabs love their children more than they hate us." In other words, in order for peace to come, the Arabs must love their children enough to stop instilling in them from childhood a hatred of Jews and the desire to die in the process of killing Jews. Only then will Arabs be able to make peace with Israel – the peace that every Israeli leader has worked for, beginning with Ben Gurion.

We are all descendants of Abraham, the Aramean. If we want to live in peace, we must love our neighbor and our brothers. We Arameans love the Jews, we see them as brothers, and we hope for the day that our fellow citizens, the Palestinian Arabs, will stop working for the destruction of Israel and its people. If we believe in God, then we must listen and live according to what the Bible tells us about Abraham and his descendants, the Jewish people. Speaking to Abraham in Genesis 12:3, God said, "I will bless those who bless you, and whoever curses you I will curse."

God bless Israel and the Jewish people.

Why Should Christians Be Zionists?

Rev. Gerald R. McDermott, Ph.D.

Rev. Dr. Gerald McDermott is an Anglican priest and serves as the Anglican Chair of Divinity at Samford University's Beeson Divinity School in Birmingham AL. A prolific author, he has written, co-written, or edited more than seventeen books and scores of articles, many of which address the subject of Christian Zionism. His most recent, *The New Christian Zionism: Fresh Perspectives on Israel and the Land* is the first-ever academic recommendation of a theology of Zionism.

The central theme of the Bible is the covenant. Not all Christians would put it this way, but all who study the Bible would agree that the central story line starts with God choosing an elderly, childless couple in what is now Iraq and declaring to them that God would use them in such a way that they and their descendants would bring blessing to the rest of the world.

Jesus and his followers claimed to be children of that couple and recipients of that blessing. Despite repeated failures among all of those descendants (except Jesus himself), the God of the Bible keeps insisting that the promise remains. God would be faithful to the promise no matter what his people do. And he would keep working with his people, using them as his partners in redeeming the world, even as they kept breaking the terms of the agreement they made with God.

The biblical word for this agreement is "covenant." On God's side it was a unilateral promise of blessing. He came to Abraham and Sarah and told them he would be their God, and they and their descendants would be his people. There were other covenants made with Noah, Moses, and David, but all of them depended on the basic covenant made with Abraham and his wife. Jesus speaks of "the blood of the covenant" (Mt 26:28; Mk 14:24), and Paul suggests that the "covenants of promise" go back to "a covenant" which "God granted to Abraham through the promise" (Eph 2:12; Gal 3:17-18).

God uses the particular (a particular person or people) to bring blessing to the universal (the world).

Some of the other covenants were conditional, but this basic Abrahamic covenant was unconditional. For example, the Mosaic covenant God made with the Jewish children of Abraham promised blessings for obedience to its terms, and punishments for disobedience (Deuteronomy 28). One of the blessings, as we shall see, was control of the land, and exile from the land was one of the punishments.

Reaching the Universal Through the Particular

Many Christians wonder why God spends so much time on the story of Israel in the Old Testament, and why this makes up three-fourths of the Christian Bible. What about the rest of the world? The New Testament contains a mission to the nations in the Great Commission. But is there anything like this in the First Testament, other than the first eleven chapters of Genesis that describe the creation and the first civilizations? Why is so much space devoted to the story of Abraham and his family, when they were such a tiny part of the rest of the world?

One of my "aha!" moments was the day I started to see that there was a pattern to the biblical story in both Testaments. The pattern moves from the particular to the universal. God uses the particular (a particular person or people) to bring blessing to the universal (the world). In the Old Testament, God uses a particular man (Abraham) and his people (the Jews) to bring blessing to their neighbors and through those neighbors to the world (the universal). The pattern is the same in the New Testament. God uses a particular man (Jesus) and his people (Jesus' Body, the Church) to bring blessing to the world.

The "ahas" kept building as I saw this pattern in the Old Testament. It starts in Genesis 12, where God calls Abraham to go to "a land that I will show you." From there God promised to make of him "a great nation," and that through him "*all the families of the earth* [would] be blessed." (vv 1- 3).

God is on mission to redeem the world (the universal) through Israel (the particular). It is not a matter of either the particular or the universal, but the universal through the particular.

This promise is repeated four more times in Genesis. Just before the destruction of Sodom and Gomorrah, God declares, "Abraham shall become a great and mighty nation, and *all the nations of the earth* shall be blessed in him" (18:18). After Abraham showed that he was willing to sacrifice his beloved son Isaac, the angel of the Lord tells him, "By your offspring shall *all the nations of the earth* gain blessing for themselves" (22:18).

Years later, famine struck and Abraham's son, Isaac, took shelter with a Philistine king. God promised Isaac that he would give him "all these lands, and *all the nations of the earth* shall gain blessing for themselves through your offspring" (26:4). When Isaac's son, Jacob, had a dream of a ladder reaching to heaven, God tells him, "You shall spread abroad to the west and to the east and to the north and to the south; and *all the families of the earth* shall be blessed in you and in your offspring" (28:14).

Throughout the Hebrew Bible, there is oscillation between the particular and the universal, but the same pattern recurs—God is on mission to redeem the world (the universal) through Israel (the particular). It is not a matter of either the particular or the universal, but the universal through the particular.

Jacob's dream of a ladder to heaven

For example, Moses told Pharaoh that God was sending the plagues in order "to make my name resound through *all the earth*" (Ex 9:16). The Lord told Moses that he would establish Israel as a holy people because then "*all the peoples on earth* shall see that you are called by the name of the Lord" (Deut 28:10). Joshua told Israel that God dried up the waters of the Jordan "so that *all the peoples of the earth* may know that the hand of the Lord is mighty" (Josh 4:24).

David told Goliath that he would strike him dead "so that *all the earth* may know that there is a God in Israel" (1 Sam 17:46). Solomon prayed the Lord would hear foreigners' prayers "so that *all the peoples of the earth* may know your name and fear you, as do your people Israel" (1 Ki 8.43).

The psalmists pray that "*all the ends of the earth* shall remember and turn to the Lord (22:27), "that your way may be known upon earth, your saving power *among all nations*" (67:2), and that "*all nations* be blessed in [Israel's king]" (72:17).[1]

Isaiah predicted a day when Israel's enemies, Egypt and Assyria (representing all the nations), will share the blessings of Israel (19:24-25). Jeremiah predicted a day when "the nations" shall hear of all the good God does for Jerusalem, and then "fear and tremble" (33:9). In Isaiah, God tells the Jewish servant of the Lord, "It is too small a thing that you should be my servant to raise up the tribes of Jacob and to restore the survivors of Israel; I will give you as a light to the nations, that my salvation may reach to the ends of the earth" (Is 49:6).

Do you see the pattern? The purpose of the covenant with Abraham and his progeny was to bless them so they in turn would bring blessing to the world. God did great things for Israel in order to educate the nations. Israel came to know God so that in turn the nations might come to know Israel's God. Hence the covenant of election was not simply soteriological (to bless and save Israel) but also missional (to bring blessing to the nations).[2]

I stumbled upon a fact that no one had ever pointed out to me: the sheer number of references to the land in the Old Testament. It was overwhelming.

This was the pattern that I came to see. It answered my question of why the story of a tiny people was the largest part of the Bible. It was all about God's way of saving the world—by raising up a little people who would be a light to the nations. I knew from the New Testament that this was the story of Jesus and the Church. And, it dawned on me about this time, that Jesus called his own church a "*little* flock" (Lk 12:32). I was starting to get it: the New Testament was continuing a story that had begun long before.

Covenant and Land

Then there was a second step in this search. The first was seeing that Israel was critical to the story of salvation for the world. God was raising up Israel as a light, and then the perfect Israelite, Jesus, as the prism through which that light would be carried by the Church to the world.

The second step was seeing something else that I had never been trained to see. This was the centrality of the land to the covenant. To me, and to most Christians, the land was an aside, a non-essential, perhaps even an unnecessary particular. Maybe, I thought, it was just another piece of the cultural baggage in the Old Testament, like the food laws, that are irrelevant to Gentile Christians.

When the biblical God calls out a people for himself, he does so in an earthy way, by making the gift of a particular land an integral aspect of that calling.

But then I stumbled upon a fact that no one had ever pointed out to me: the sheer number of references to the land in the Old Testament. It was overwhelming. As the great biblical scholar Gerhard von Rad put it, "Of all the promises made to the patriarchs it was that of the land that was the most prominent and decisive."[3]

1 For more of this theme in the psalms, see Ps. 86.9 and 145.12.

2 Christopher J. H. Wright, *The Mission of God: Unblocking the Bible's Grand Narrative* (Downer's Grove: IVP Academic, 2006).

3 Gerhard von Rad, *The Problem of the Hexateuch and Other Essays* (London: Oliver and Boys, 1966), 79.

By one scholar's count, land is the fourth most frequent noun or substantive in the Hebrew Bible. He notes that it is more dominant statistically than the idea of covenant.[4] By my count, the land (*eretz*) of Israel is either stated or implied more than one thousand times in the Old Testament. Of the 250 times that covenant (*b'rit*) is mentioned, in 70 percent of those instances (177 times) covenant is either directly or indirectly connected to the land of Israel. Of the 74 times that *b'rit* appears in Torah (the Pentateuch), 73 percent of those times (54) include the gift of the land, either explicitly or implicitly.

In other words, when the biblical God calls out a people for himself, he does so in an earthy way, by making the gift of a particular land an integral aspect of that calling.

Book	**Covenant+Land Explicit (Both Words)**	**C+L Explicit Total**	**C+L Implicit (Land Used, Covenant Implied)**	**Covenant Alone (God's Covenant with Israel)**	**Covenant Alone (total)**
Genesis	5	6	70	13	17
Exodus	3	5	105	7	8
Leviticus	3	3	45	4	4
Numbers	0	0	98	3	5
Deuteronomy	3	3	129	13	23
Torah	**14**	**17**	**447**	**40**	**57**
Joshua	3	4	64	14	15
Judges	2	2	14	1	2
Ruth	0	0	0	0	0
1 Samuel	1	1	2	0	6
2 Samuel	0	1	9	1	2
1 Kings	2	2	19	3	8
2 Kings	0	0	28	9	10
1 Chronicles	0	0	12	6	11
2 Chronicles	1	1	29	6	14
Ezra	0	0	8	0	1
Nehemiah	1	1	13	2	2
Esther	0	0	0	0	0
Job	0	0	0	0	2
Psalms	2	2	67	18	19
Proverbs	0	0	15	0	1
Ecclesiastes	0	0	0	0	0
Song of Solomon	0	0	0	0	0
Other	**12**	**14**	**280**	**60**	**93**

4 Elmer A. Martens, *God's Design: A Focus on Old Testament Theology* (Grand Rapids: Baker, 1981), 97-98.

Book	Covenant+Land Explicit (Both Words)	C+L Explicit Total	C+L Implicit (Land Used, Covenant Implied)	Covenant Alone (God's Covenant with Israel)	Covenant Alone (total)
Isaiah	2	2	74	7	10
Jeremiah	4	4	104	11	17
Lamentations	0	0	0	0	0
Ezekiel	2	3	56	11	13
Daniel	1	1	4	3	5
Hosea	1	1	8	2	4
Joel	0	0	5	0	0
Amos	0	0	6	1	1
Obadiah	0	0	0	0	0
Jonah	0	0	0	0	0
Micah	0	0	4	0	0
Nahum	0	0	0	0	0
Habakkuk	0	0	2	0	0
Zephaniah	0	0	2	0	0
Haggai	0	0	0	0	0
Zechariah	0	0	13	1	2
Malachi	0	0	0	5	6
Prophets	**10**	**11**	**278**	**41**	**58**
Total	**36**	**42**	**1005**	**141**	**208**

Tables compiled by Benjamin Cowgill

According to the *Dictionary of Biblical Imagery,* "Next to God himself, the longing for land dominates all others [in the Old Testament]." Land is presented by Torah as a place of spiritual testing, and its pollution by sin and Israel's consequent exiles are portrayed as analogous to humanity's fall from grace in Eden and consequent expulsion. Adam, formed from land, failed to protect it and therefore allowed the serpent (evil) access to it. Land also represents the human condition: "Good in principle, land is cursed as a result of humanity's sin, and people are alienated from it as well as being joined to it." [5]

Possession is Conditional

It is this note of possible alienation that is sometimes missed in both scholarly and non-scholarly treatments of biblical Zionism. The first five books of the Bible specify that the covenantal promise of the land does not *guarantee* possession of the land, but that control of the land depends on moral and religious conditions.

Jack Schechter has shown in his study of Deuteronomy – which was probably written as Jews were *re*-possessing the land after exile from the land – that continued possession of the land

5 *Dictionary of Biblical Imagery*, eds. Leland Ryken, James C. Wilhoit, Tremper Longman III (Downers Grove: InterVarsity Press, 1998), 487-88.

was dependent on Israel's faithfulness to the covenant. As Deuteronomy 19:8-9 says: the Lord "gives you all the land which he promised to give to your fathers—provided you are *careful to keep all this commandment*" [added emphasis in Schechter's translation][6]

So the First Testament never guaranteed eternal possession of the land. It made possession conditional upon faithfulness to God.

Keeping the Title Even When Under Discipline

But if possession of the land was never guaranteed, *title* to the land was. The prophets wrote that even during those times when Israel's disobedience caused the land to be forfeited, it was still theirs. While in exile, Jeremiah wrote that God was promising to "bring them [the people of Israel] back to *their own land that I gave to their ancestors*" (Jer. 16:15; 12: 14-17).

God's gift of a land to Abraham's progeny was forever, even if their enjoyment of the gift was restricted to certain periods of history.

God told Ezekiel that he had driven the people of Israel off "*their own soil*" because "they defiled it with their ways and their deeds; their conduct in my sight was like the uncleanness of a woman in her menstrual period." This was why he "scattered them among the nations." But there was coming a time when "I will take you from the nations, and gather you from all the countries, and bring you into *your own land*" (Ezek 36:17-19, 24). One scholar sums up this dynamic as follows:

> Israel might and in fact did lose the land, because of failure on their part to live in the land in loyalty to Yahweh. Yet the land was inalienable in the sense that it could not be forcibly taken from Israel. Israel, however, through disobedience, forfeited the land. Prophets in the exile fell back on the inalienable right of Israel to the land, and announced a return from exile to the land, for, they said, it was rightfully theirs still. [7]

The reason why the title could be forever when possession was not is because there were different covenants that depended on the central Abrahamic covenant. As I mentioned at the beginning, the Abrahamic covenant was the basic covenant to which both Jesus and Paul refer. It was unconditional. God said to Israel that he would always be their God and he was giving them a land to be theirs forever.

Jews praying at the Western Wall in the 1870's.

However, the Mosaic covenant stipulated that *enjoyment* of the land and other blessings was conditional upon Israel's obedience. This is why the covenant God made with Abraham was full of "I will" promises, but the covenant with Moses was full of "you must" requirements. The promise to Abraham was that God *will* give his family a land forever. But the promise to Moses was that Abraham's family *must* obey God's commandments if she wants to stay on the land.

6 Jack Shechter, *The Land of Israel: It's Theological Dimensions* (Lanham: University Press of America, 2010).
7 Elmer Martins, *God's Design: A Focus on Old Testament Theology* (Grand Rapids: Baker, 1981), 106.

The Abrahamic covenant was unconditional, while the Mosaic covenant was conditional. God's gift of a land to Abraham's progeny was forever, even if their enjoyment of the gift was restricted to certain periods of history.

Do the New Promises Cancel Out the Old?

Many Christians wonder, however, why this even matters if God has moved on. In other words, if God has made new promises about a whole world, how could the promises concerning the land of Israel still hold? After all, didn't the prophets predict that the reign of Israel's messiah would be over the whole world?

Indeed, some Christians have made this very argument. They have assumed that because Isaiah, for example, predicted that God would use the servant of the Lord to bring "salvation to the whole earth," and that kings would "prostrate themselves" before the messiah (49:6-7), that God in the messianic age would no longer be concerned with the land of Israel. According to supercessionism (the view that the Church has superseded Israel), these new promises about the whole world cancelled out the old promises about the tiny country of Israel.

God is perfectly capable of honoring both sets of promises.

However, there is no reason why new promises must override old ones. The prophets don't assume this. They expanded the promised inheritance of God's people beyond the definable boundaries of Canaan to include the world, but they retained their expectation that Israel would return to the land of Palestine.

In other words, in the writings of the prophets we find new promises for the messiah and his worldwide reign, but these new promises do not overrule the earlier promises of a particular land for a particular people. "Expansion [of the promise] is not synonymous with abrogation."[8] Just as Abraham was to be the father of Israel *and* many nations, so too Israel would return to her own land *and* the rest of God's people would live in a whole world.

God is perfectly capable of honoring both sets of promises. After all, this is in keeping with his pattern of achieving the universal through the particular. God has always wanted to bring salvation to the whole world, and has always used particular persons and a particular people (Israel) to do that. For him to make promises about the whole world was simply his way of showing *how* he would use Israel – which, as we read in the New or Second Testament, is embodied by the perfect Israelite.

Promise of Return

The prophets, as we have seen, wrote mostly from exile, and prophesied that one day Jews from all over the world would return to the land. Isaiah, for example, predicted in the early seventh century BCE that in some future day, God "will assemble the banished of Israel, and gather the dispersed of Judah from the four corners of the earth" (11.12).

Roughly one century later Jeremiah wrote that "the days are coming" when it shall be said that the Lord "brought [the people of Israel] out of all the countries where he had driven them . . . back to their own land that [he] gave to their fathers. . . There they shall dwell in their own land" (16.14-15; 23.8).

8 McComiskey, 205.

Ezekel's vision of the Valley of Dry Bones

In the early sixth century BCE, Ezekiel repeatedly prophesied the ingathering of all the scattered Israelites back to the land. His famous vision of the dry bones is an explicit prophecy of return to the land. As it says in Ezekiel 37: "I will put my spirit within you, and you shall live, and I will place you on your own soil."

Two chapters later there is a description of a return that will be a restoration. The exiles at that point will be prosperous and secure, without fear. "I will restore the fortunes of Jacob . . .They shall forget their shame, and all the treachery they have practiced against me, when they live securely in their land with no one to make them afraid" (Ez 39:25-26).

Later in that century, Zechariah delivered God's promise that "though I scattered them among the nations, yet in far countries they shall remember me, and with their children they shall live and return" (Zech. 10:9). Similar promises are made throughout the prophets over the course of different periods in Israel's later history – after the first exile to Assyria, during and after the second exile to Babylon, and after the return of the exiles under Ezra and Nehemiah.

Some scholars have suggested that these prophecies of return were fulfilled when some of the Babylonian exiles returned to rebuild Jerusalem toward the end of the sixth century BCE. But there's a problem with that interpretation, which is that, Jesus and the apostles were still expecting a future return. They seem to have believed that a new restoration still lay in the future.

Zionism in the New Testament

When Jesus quotes Isaiah's prediction that the Temple would become "a house of prayer for all nations" (Mark 11.17; Is. 56.1), he seems to concur, as Richard Hays suggests, with Isaiah's vision of "an eschatologically restored Jerusalem" where foreigners would come to God's holy mountain to join the "outcasts of Israel" whom God has "gathered" (Is 56.7-8). [9]

Hays adds that John's figural reading of Jesus' body as the new temple (John 2.21) "should be read neither as flatly supersessionist nor as hostile to continuity with Israel."[10] It does not deny the literal sense of Israel's Scriptures—that the Temple was God's house—"but completes it by linking it typologically with the narrative of Jesus and disclosing a deeper prefigurative truth within the literal historical sense."[11]

These repeated references to the twelve tribes imply restoration of Israel, particularly in Jerusalem.

In Matthew 19 Jesus tells his disciples that "in the new world, when the Son of Man shall sit on his glorious throne, you who have followed me will also sit on twelve thrones, judging the twelve tribes of Israel" (v. 28). James Sanders has observed that these repeated references to the twelve tribes imply restoration of Israel, particularly in Jerusalem. [12]

9 Richard Hays, *Reading Backwards: Figural Christology and the Fourfold Gospel Witness* (Waco: Baylor University Press, 2014), 6-7.
10 Ibid., 102.
11 Ibid.
12 James Sanders, *Jesus and Judaism* (Philadelphia: Fortress, 1985), 98.

The Gospel of Luke records Anna speaking of the baby Jesus "to all who were waiting for the redemption of Jerusalem" (Luke 2.38), and Jesus' expectation that when he returns, Israel will welcome him. "You will not see me again until you say, 'Blessed is he who comes in the name of the Lord'" (Lk 13.34-35; Matt 23.37-39). Luke suggests that this return will occur in Jerusalem (Lk 21.24-28).

When his disciples asked Jesus just before his ascension, "Lord, are you at this time going to restore the kingdom to Israel?" (Acts 1.6), Jesus did not challenge their assumption that one day the kingdom would be restored to physical Israel. He simply said the Father had set the date, and they did not need to know it yet.

Zionism is all through the New Testament. The only reason we have not seen it is because we have been trained not to see it.

It was these sorts of indications in the gospels and Acts that caused Markus Bockmuehl to write, "the early Jesus movement evidently continued to focus upon the restoration of Israel's twelve tribes in a new messianic kingdom."[13]

Paul, Peter, and the writer of the book of Revelation had similar expectations. Paul uses Isaiah's prophecy of restoration in chapter 59 to declare that "The deliverer will come from Zion, he will banish ungodliness from Jacob" (Rom 11.26). In Acts 3, Peter looks forward to "the times of restoration of all things which God spoke through the mouth of his holy prophets from ancient time" (Acts 3.21).[14]

The word Peter uses for "restoration" is the same word (*apokatastasis*) used in the Septuagint (which the early church used as its Bible) for God's future return of Jews from all over the world to Israel.[15] In Revelation the Lamb draws his followers to Zion in the final stage of history (12.1), and the new earth is centered in Jerusalem, which has twelve gates named after "the twelve tribes of the sons of Israel" (Rev 21.2, 12).

There was always a remnant of Christians who saw a future for Israel.

Zionism is all through the New Testament. The only reason we have not seen it is because we have been trained not to see it. Supercessionism has been the dominant Christian interpretation concerning the future of Israel for most of the last two thousand years.

Zionism in the History of Christianity

But a new thing is happening in the Church. We are now realizing that there was always a Christian remnant that saw a future for Israel, both as a people and as a land. Even the Church Fathers, many of whom often taught a kind of replacement theology, nevertheless saw a future for Israel.

Justin Martyr (100-165), for example, expected that the millennium would be centered in Jerusalem. He wrote:

---

13 Markus Bockmuehl, *Jewish Law in Gentile Churches: Halakhah and the Beginning of Christian Public Ethics* (Grand Rapids: Baker Academic, 2000), xi.

14 In this and other biblical quotations, I use my own translations from the Hebrew and Greek, unless otherwise noted.

15 Jer 16.15 I will bring them back [apokataste-so] their own land that I gave to their fathers; Jer 24.6 I will set my eyes on them for good, and I will bring them back [apokataste-so] to this land; Jer 50 [27 LXX]. 19 I will restore Israel [apokataste-so] to his pasture; Hos 11.11 They shall come trembling like birds from Egypt, and like doves from the land of Assyria, and I will return [apokataste-so] them to their homes, declares the LORD.

> But I and others, who are right-minded Christians on all points, are assured that there will be a resurrection of the dead, and a thousand years in Jerusalem, which will then be built, adorned and enlarged, [as] the prophets Ezekiel and Isaiah and others declare . . .

Tertullian (160 – c.225) thought that God punished the Jews by tearing "from [their] throat[s] . . . the very land of promise," but still believed that they would one day be returned to their land.

Justin Martyr, 100-165 CE

A bit later in the third century, the Egyptian bishop Nepos, who "was a respected and admired Christian leader," foresaw a restoration of Jerusalem and rebuilding of the temple. Millennial teaching was prevalent in that area of third-century Egypt, and had been so for a long time, along with, presumably, faith in a restored Israel.[16]

Nevertheless, once Augustine's amillennial eschatology became accepted in the medieval church, with its assertion that the millennium is simply the rule of Christ through the existing Church, few medieval thinkers saw a future for the people or land of Israel. All Old Testament prophecies of future Israel were interpreted as predictions of the Christian Church, established after the resurrection of Christ.

Augustine of Hippo, 354-430 CE

There were exceptions, however. Joachim of Fiore (c. 1135-1202) and others predicted a return of Jews to their land in a future age of the Spirit.[17] But it was not until the Reformation and later, that renewed vision for a future Israel gained momentum.

As early as the sixteenth century, the stimulus for a new kind of Zionism came from Britain through the publication of three books. The first was the Geneva Bible, first published in 1560 and more popular than the King James Bible for generations. The notes for Romans 11 predict that one day Israel as a people "shall embrace Christ" and then "the worlde shal be restored to a newe life."

Cover of *Pilgrim's Progress*

John Bale's (1495-1563), *The Image of Both Churches*, published by Thomas East in 1570, also included hope for the national conversion of Jews to Protestantism, and assigned to them a place at the throne of the Lamb at the end of history.

John Foxe's *Book of Martyrs* (1563), which was the most widely read book in English for several centuries after the Bible, and John Bunyan's *Pilgrim's Progress*, both assured their readers that God's promises to Jews are "remaining still in their force."

In the 17th century British thinkers, especially the Puritans, started predicting a Jewish return to Zion. Some thought Jews would return to the land without converting to Christianity first. This belief became so

16 Robert L. Wilken, *The Land Called Holy: Palestine in Christian History and Thought* (New Haven: Yale University Press, 1992), 76-77, drawing on Eusebius, The History of the Church 7.24 and other sources.
17

widespread that you see it in John Milton who, in *Paradise Regained,* wrote of the return of the people of Israel to their ancient land.

Most of this modern Zionism came before the mid-19th century and most was postmillennialist. This is important to note because modern scholarship has declared that Christian Zionism originated in the mid-19th century and is rooted in premillennial dispensationalism. But, both of these statements are wrong. In fact, Christian Zionism has been around for 2000 years and the vast majority of Christian Zionists have had nothing to do with dispensationalism.

Christian Zionism has been around for 2000 years and the vast majority of Christian Zionists have had nothing to do with dispensationalism.

Conclusion

Christian Zionism is the only thing that makes sense of the one story of covenant that runs like a red thread throughout the Bible. It is the story of how the God of the cosmos saves a sinful world through a particular people. God created people of flesh, in whom he incarnated himself, first in the people of Israel and then in one Israelite. He promised this people a land and peoplehood, through which salvation would come to the world.

God is still in the process of saving the world through this particular people and land, as individuals are joined to this God of Israel and the people of Israel through the Israelite, Jesus. God promised to return his people, Israel, to the land of Israel, and to make Jerusalem the center of the world to come. And, just as God has kept his promise to return his people to the land, he will keep his promise to make this land the center of the new heaven and the new earth.

Antidote for the Threat to Evangelical Support of Israel: A Renewal of Leadership within the Church

Rev. Petra Heldt, Ph.D.

Rev. Dr. Petra Heldt is a faculty member of Jerusalem University College, the University of the Holy Land in Jerusalem, and the Rothberg International School at Hebrew University, Jerusalem. Petra is also the General Secretary of the Ecumenical Theological Research Fraternity in Israel, founded in 1966 to be a catalyst in Christian-Jewish dialogue, for the purpose of deepening the Christian relationship with Jews, Judaism and Israel.

The vast majority of Evangelical and faithful Protestant lay people typically maintain a pro-Israel position. There are Church hierarchs, however, who target these historical supporters of the Jewish State for the purpose of turning their support away from Israel. But there is an antidote to this problem, and that is a renewal of leadership within the Church.

The threat to Evangelical support of Israel by a Church hierarchy that cooperates with the anti-Israel policies of organizations such as the World Council of Churches must be resisted. This resistance is not meant to be anarchic. It is meant to establish responsible new leadership. Therefore, I have invented the term *resistance-cum-leadership* to emphasize the need for renewed leadership, and to prevent the misunderstanding that I am against Church leadership in general.

After analyzing recent and current Church leadership, I will propose strategies to counter the threat to traditional Evangelical support for Israel, demonstrating how resistance-cum-leadership can be an effective remedy. I propose a permanent mechanism, using both short-term and long-term tools, to establish and maintain *resistance-cum-leadership.*

Church Hierarchy at the Time of the Shoah and Beyond

Traditional Church order dictates that the hierarchy leads the faithful. At the time of the Shoah, some Protestant leaders provided leadership that demonstrated sympathy for the plight of the Jews, but the majority of Church hierarchs cooperated with anti-Jewish Nazi politics. In the decades following the Shoah, Church hierarchs not only cooperated with the anti-Jewish Arab-Euro alignment, but also hijacked theology that included a biblical belief in a future for Israel.

Just as there was resistance to anti-Jewish Nazi politics within the Church by leaders such as Dietrich Bonhoeffer, there is resistance to the cooperation of Church hierarchs with the anti-Jewish Arab-Euro alignment. Resistance did and does exist, but in most cases, it lacked and continues to lack leadership. As a result, we see the continued take-over of the Church by those who oppose an Israel-inclusive theology and Jewish-Christian relations – to the point that now, Church hierarchs and the Western-Arab alignment have captured members of the Evangelical leadership as well.

> *"Silence in the face of evil is itself evil: God will not hold us guiltless. Not to speak is to speak. Not to act is to act."*
>
> -Dietrich Bonhoeffer

In response to this erosion of traditional Christian support for Israel and Jewish-Christian relations, remnants of Evangelical leadership and faithful Protestants have formed a *resistance-cum-leadership*, and to a large extent, the faithful are now leading Church hierarchy. A significant source of encouragement for resistance to Church hierarchy on the part of the faithful came from Jews in response to the massive failure of the European Church hierarchy at the time of the Shoah.

Elie Wiesel, Professor, Nobel Laurieate, and Holocaust Survivor

It was men like Jules Isaac, Eli Wiesel, Yehuda Ashkenazi, Peter Levinson, and David Flusser who re-directed the Church and stipulated a reclamation of the Jewish roots of Christian theology. In response, many of the faithful rejected two traditional cornerstones of Christian theology: the belief that the Church has superseded Israel, and the practice of proselytizing Jews.

However, there are still two issues that continue to have a long-term, negative impact on traditional support for Israel. The first is that Israel studies remain underdeveloped, which results in a lack of convincing arguments against proselytizing Jews and against supersessionism. The second is that a weak Church hierarchy is ruled by Church academics who continue to teach supersessionism, and by Church bureaucrats who stop people in the pews from engaging in any kind of pro-Israel action. The developing Arab-European alignment in Churches has exploited both issues, expressed in the form of Palestinian Replacement Theology.

Palestinian Replacement Theology

The development of Palestinian replacement theology, which began in 1967, is an important pseudo-theological tool used by the Arab world in its efforts to turn Western Churches against Israel in favor of the Palestinian cause. This faulty theology has been significantly advanced through the efforts of the Sabeel Institute in Jerusalem under the leadership of Naim Ateek. Palestinian replacement theology makes particular inroads in Churches with hierarchs who are attempting to be trendy, and with reactionary hierarchs who already believe in supersessionism.

Palestinian replacement theology became an essential component of the rapprochement between the Euro-Arab political and economic bloc and the West.

Much of the European Protestant hierarchy (academic and bureaucratic) is connected to para-Church superstructures such as the World Council of Churches (WCC). The WCC frequently promotes new political fashions, and one of the most significant trends in the 1970's was the Arab-European rapprochement between Western and Muslim countries – a rapprochement characterized by *Judeophobia* and *Islamophilia*.

The Arab-European policy developed in tandem with reactionary theology. Trendy Protestant hierarchs accepted Palestinian replacement theology and hijacked Jewish-Christian relations even as they embraced *Islamophilia*. In this way, Palestinian replacement theology became an essential component of the rapprochement between the Euro-Arab political and economic bloc and the West.

In 1977, a Euro-Arab Seminar sponsored by *Instituto per l'Oriente* in Rome and the Arabic literature section of the University of Venice adopted recommendations for the establishment of Euro-Arab cultural centers to spread the Arab language and teach about Islamic culture. At the subsequent Hamburg Symposium in 1983, the Arab delegates reminded their European colleagues that they must teach about the eminence and supremacy of Islamic civilization and religion at the university level.

Rev. Naim Ateek, Palestinian Replacement Theologian

A leading Palestinian replacement theologian, Naim Ateek, contributed significantly to this project by supplying an applicable version of supersessionist doctrine. His doctoral dissertation, *Justice and Only Justice* (published by Orbis Books in 1989), made supersessionism fashionable.

Palestinian replacement theology was also in line with the 1974 Lahore Summit of the Organization of the Islamic Conference where Secretary General al-Tahomi commended the Churches in Arab countries and worldwide on behalf of the Palestinians and praised their backing of Arab sovereignty over Jerusalem. His address conformed to the Quranic dogma of Islam's precedence over Judaism and Christianity. Again, trendy Protestant hierarchs followed suit and promoted this erroneous doctrine.

The supersessionism of Palestinian replacement theology rests on three foundations: the re-writing of history, dualism, and Gnosticism. Under this system of historical revisionism, history starts and ends with Islam/Palestinianism, which results in the beliefs that Judaism and Christianity are based on Islam, a Jewish Temple never existed in Jerusalem, Jesus was a Palestinian, and the land of Israel is rightfully the land of Palestine.

This renewed support for Israel constituted a formidable threat to the political concept of a Western-Arab alignment, which meant that the pro-Israel movement had to be stopped.

The foundation of dualism purports that Islam/Palestinianism represents the bright and the moral, while Judaism represents the dark and immoral. Judaism is falsely presented as the motive force behind Jewish theft of land, the killing of children, the poisoning of wells, and the corruption of the international community.

Gnosticism, which promotes enhanced or esoteric knowledge, believes that what appears is not true, the hidden is the real thing, and the real thing is not real. This belief system allows Palestinian theology to replace Isaac with Ishmael; Jesus with Judas as the victim of crucifixion; and the text of the Bible – which is considered faulty – with the superior text of Islam/Palestinianism.

Evangelical Leadership and the Faithful Versus the Western-Arab Alignment

In the 1980's and 90's, Evangelical leaders and faithful Protestants began to oppose anti-Biblical hierarchs by exposing the error of Palestinian replacement theology and advocating in favor of the Jewish State. The combination of the teaching of anti-replacement theology and a pro-Israel attitude nurtured support for the Jewish State in the Western world.

This renewed support for Israel constituted a formidable threat to the political concept of a Western-Arab alignment, which meant that the pro-Israel movement had to be stopped. The task was given to politically savvy Palestinian replacement theology activists. Two strategies were adopted to hijack support for Israel: contempt for and flattery of Evangelical leaders, based respectively on their support or rejection of Israel.

The issue of proselytizing Jews has undermined good relations between Jews and faithful supporters of Israel.

Defenders of the Western-Arab alignment employ two main tactics to create contempt for Israel supporters. First of all, Evangelical leaders are ridiculed for their allegedly unsophisticated reading of the Bible, and condemned for translating it into support of Israel. And secondly, these leaders' unconditional love for Israel is juxtaposed with Israel's alleged apartheid system. These false charges create allies for the Palestinian cause from within Evangelical leadership, and sideline others who don't join the crusade.

Teaching contempt for Israel supporters comes from three kinds of adversaries: Protestant and Catholic Christians who oppose Israel for political reasons, secular Jews who oppose Israel for political reasons, and religious Jews who oppose Christian support of Israel due to their concern over Christian proselytization of Jews. These adversaries all cooperate with Palestinian representatives in opposition to the pro-Israel position held by Evangelical leadership and other faithful Protestants.

The false charges that encourage contempt also prompt the exclusion of Israel supporters from opportunities and from spheres of influence. For example, Israel supporters are often prevented from entering Church hierarchies and from participating in Western-sponsored programs abroad. Within Israel, pro-Israeli Christians are frequently regarded as leaning towards Israel's political right, which is unpopular with left wing Israelis who dominate academia. And sometimes, Zionist Christians are suspected as having ulterior motives, and this makes Israeli government officials uncomfortable.

In 1989, Evangelical critics of Israel from around the world gathered at the Willowbank Christian Resort in Bermuda to discuss the question of proselytizing Jews and issued a paper on the Jews' alleged need of the Messiah. According to James Rudin of the American Jewish Committee, that attitude is "a blueprint for a spiritual genocide of the Jewish people."

Palestinian replacement theologians had two objectives when they initiated their agenda in 1967 and through patient consistency, they have realized much success.

Religious and secular Jews alike reacted with hostility, and ever since, the issue of proselytizing Jews has undermined good relations between Jews and faithful supporters of Israel. Religious Jews reject Evangelicals as a security threat, secular Jews oust Evangelicals as political foes, and Palestinian replacement theology hierarchs treat Evangelicals as objects of hate. The subject of proselytization is the one subject for which religious Jews, secular Jews, and Palestinian theologians join forces, and as a result, Evangelicals have become a punching ball for everyone.

Since 1989, Evangelical leadership has been hit hard and ostracized by both Jewish and Christian adversaries. In an attempt to remove themselves as objects of contempt, some

Dr. Gary Burge, Professor at Wheaton College

leaders have supported and embraced the proselytizing of Jews and aligned themselves with the proponents of Palestinian replacement theology. As a result, these leaders have gone from being ostracized to being the recipients of recognition and favorable attention.

Among the first Evangelicals to respond positively to the Palestinian movement were people like Dr. Gary Burge of Wheaton College in Illinois, and Tony Campolo, a popular progressive Evangelical leader and author. They were soon followed by entire communities, such as the Willow Creek Community Church, headquartered in Chicago, IL, and branches of academic institutions like Wheaton College.

Palestinian replacement theologians had two objectives when they initiated their agenda in 1967 and through patient consistency, they have realized much success. The first objective was to turn Evangelical leadership from being pro-Israel to being pro-Palestinian. As a result of their persistence, the threat to future Evangelical support of Israel is more real today than ever before.

The second objective of the Palestinian movement was to encourage the proselytization of Jews, but not Moslems. Of course, proselytization of Moslems is dangerous – so it is easier to avoid it. Proselytizing Jews is not dangerous, *and* it damages relations between Christians and Jews because of the Jewish concern that it will result in the elimination of the Jewish people. Therefore, targeting Jews for evangelization furthers the Palestinian objective of separating Jews and Christian supporters of Israel.

Resistance-cum-leadership as an Antidote for the Current Threat

The preceding analysis of recent and current Church leadership shows that anti-Israelism within the Church reoccurs regularly and works to obliterate pro-Israel elements from within.

The following discussion focuses on remedies for the threat to Israel supporters and a strategy for preserving *resistance-cum-leadership*, which can serve as an effective antidote to the current threat.

Israel faces anti-Israelism in every generation. So do Evangelical and Protestant churches. But Christians are not prepared to fight anti-Israel agendas because of classical anti-Judaism within the Church system. Therefore, a permanent mechanism is required that will strengthen *resistance-cum-leadership* through the implementation of methods that provide both short-term and long-term effects.

Establishment of an Action Center

One method that would have an immediate impact, as well as provide long-term effects, would be the establishment of an action center modeled upon existing joint ventures between Jews and Christians. The center would focus on three areas of activism: 1) pro-Israel advocacy for Jews and Christians through print and social media, and through lobbying in churches, politics, education, and culture; 2) the advancement of pro-Israel Jews and Christians for leadership positions in the public arena, for awards given by social, political, artistic and religious circles, for grants, and for all other relevant fields of influence; and 3) the development and implementation of pro-active challenges to attackers of Israel, such as those recommended by Malcolm Lowe in his chapter.

Long-term effects would also be achieved through methods that strengthen *resistance-cum-leadership*. These include the pursuit of three areas of study by Jewish and Christian scholars working in tandem: studies of the Bible in the Land of Israel, studies of Christian mission, and studies of biblical ethics.

Studies of the Bible in the Land of the Bible

Studies of the Bible in the Land of Israel by both Jewish and Christian scholars working together is essential in order for the Jewishness of the Christian faith to be emphasized.

These studies are necessary in order to re-introduce Jewish space into Christian studies of the biblical text and must include the following aspects: the existential realism of the text as revealed by synchronisms of language and landscape; the symphony of written law (Tanach) and Oral Law (the tradition of the Sages); and reading the Bible with a memory older than history. To read the Bible with a memory older than history means to keep in mind the oral tradition that predates written tradition. In the Western world, oral tradition – the memory – is not as highly respected as written manuscripts and historic documents. However, in many parts of the Middle East, oral tradition is much more highly valued because it is considered immutable.

One program already created for the purpose of enabling Jewish and Christian scholars to study the Bible together in Israel is the annual International Bible Study Week in Jerusalem organized by the Ecumenical Theological Research Fraternity in Israel.

Studies of Christian Mission

Studies of Christian mission are necessary for the purpose of re-investigating Christian relations with Israel. To advance such studies, two points, in particular, should be made clear. The first is the necessity for Christians to recognize that Jews experienced Christian proselytization as a curse, and that the Church sinned when employing mission as a tool for abuse.

In 1981, at the Ecumenical Theological Research Fraternity on the notion of "Mission to Jews?" Malcolm Lowe suggested that any contemporary proselytization of Jews must be treated in the light of the rabbinic conception of *hora'at sha'ah*. This means that Christian mission must be suspended for the foreseeable future. Jews will appreciate it, and Christians can make use of this time as an opportunity for repentance.

The second point is an understanding of the fact that the command to proselytize in Matthew 28 is connected to the idea of holiness. In this text, a Jewish Messiah instructs his Jewish followers to make holy the entire *present world* for the coming of the Messiah.

The process of holiness (Leviticus 17) is key for humankind in the presence of God. Jesus' instruction concerning bringing holiness to the Gentile world follows the example of Joseph bringing it to Egypt, Ezekiel to Persia, Philo to the Greeks, and Second Century BCE Jews to the Edomites in the south of Israel and to the Itureans (predecessors of the Druze) on Mount Hermon in the north.

By way of contrast, the Apostle Paul connects mission with the notion of salvation in Romans 9-11. In this text, Jesus, the Jewish Messiah, is the objective reality for the forgiveness of sins for all and thus provides salvation for all mankind in the *coming world.* This contributes to the rabbinic discussion reported in Mishna Sanhedrin 10 where it says that, all Israel has a share in the world to come.

Ever since the early Church, these two notions – holiness in this world and salvation in the world to come – have often been interconnected. Indeed, in the books of the New Testament, mission is a notion with two separate but equal values, holiness and salvation. Contemporary studies of mission need to consider the significance and impact of both.

Studies of Biblical Ethics

The third area of study that needs to be pursued by Jewish and Christian scholars working in tandem is that of biblical ethics. A study of ethics for the sake of rejecting anti-Semitism and anti-Israelism needs to include at least the four following aspects.

1) Programs for teaching about love of one's enemy must be developed and implemented. Evangelicals who have started to follow the teaching of Palestinian replacement theologians can be regained through the teaching of love for the other – specifically Israel.

2) Programs for teaching the differences between Torah and Greco-Roman law must be revised. Torah is law that establishes social order, while Greco-Roman law establishes political power. These opposing systems of law can be re-evaluated in light of Western values and systems of law.

3) The notion of leadership must be examined, together with the nature of power and authority. Such studies would probe the question of how to be a leader while living with ethical standards in the face of threats and fashionable trends.

4) Solutions for the problem of religious violence and extremism in the name of God must be investigated. This study would look at the notions of reconciliation and forgiveness in the context of violence and the exploitation of human beings.

This list is just a start. Additional subjects can be added to this area of study, as necessary. Such studies will help to stabilize *resistance-cum-leadership* as an effective antidote to the current threat to Evangelical support for Israel. As a result, Evangelical leadership and faithful Protestants will be strengthened in their commitment to support Israel, and Jewish and Christian lives will be protected.

Compelling Reasons for Jewish-Evangelical Cooperation in Support of Israel

The Jewish Roots of Christianity

Brad H. Young, Ph.D.

Dr. Brad Young is professor of Biblical Literature in the School of Theology and Ministry at Oral Roberts University in Tulsa, OK. He earned his PhD from Hebrew University, Jerusalem with a specialization in New Testament Studies and the Jewish beginnings of Christianity. In addition to his academic focus on the Jewish roots of Christianity, Brad is active in interfaith dialogue and works to build bridges between the Jewish and Christian faith communities.

I thank CAMERA for their excellent journalism and objective reporting that challenges the prevailing bias of the media – a bias that demonizes Israel through the presentation of a false narrative. In a time when reporters tend to spin a story to follow that narrative, it is inspiring to see how CAMERA journalists present the facts. In particular, CAMERA's Christian media analysts are currently working to expose a carefully calculated move within evangelical Christianity to disengage from Scriptural teachings that uphold the eternal covenantal relationship between God and the Jewish people.

A legacy of hatred, anti-Semitism, anti-Zionism, and replacement theology is being renewed through an agenda that intends to transform evangelical Christian faith and practice. In the process, the achievements of Israeli democracy are vilified while the message of hate from Fatah, Hamas, Islamic State, and Iran is proliferated. As a result, Jews and Christians are being attacked both politically and physically.

Palestinian leaders envision a Palestinian state completely free of Jews.

Palestinian leaders routinely provoke their citizens into violence against Israeli citizens. But too often, their public incitements are either ignored or justified. Instead, the victims of terror are blamed as the cause of terrorism in the perverted moral equivalency of the news media. CAMERA is calling attention to this media distortion, and to the disturbing movement within the Evangelical world that seeks to align Christian teachings with the fallacious narrative perpetuated by the media.

One example of the spurious narrative promoted by Christians is the failure to recognize that Jesus was a Jew. Organizations such as the Christ at the Checkpoint conference in Bethlehem purport that Jesus was a Palestinian. Consistent with this belief, Palestinian Christians ignore the fact that the holy family would not be permitted entry into the Bethlehem of today because Fatah prohibits Jews from entering territory under its control.

It is actually difficult to be against the Jewish people when you understand that the founder of your faith was Jewish.

Indeed, Palestinian leaders envision a Palestinian state completely free of Jews. This is in marked contrast to the rich diversity of population that characterizes the modern State of Israel.

In contrast to the religious prejudice and violence so prevalent in today's Middle East, the democratic State of Israel continues to be a haven of religious freedom for her Christian and Muslim citizens, as well as the Jewish faithful. Christians living in Nazareth under Israeli democracy are living in paradise compared to Christians in Gaza City under Hamas, or Christians in Bethlehem under Fatah and Hamas, or Christians living in Baghdad.

This is especially significant now, as U.S. congressional leaders of both parties acknowledge that a genocide of Christians is currently taking place in the Middle East, particularly wherever the Islamic State is in control. And the Islamic State is already operative in Gaza City and Ramallah, threatening to attack Israel next.

Christianity and Her Jewish Roots

What are the Jewish roots of Christianity? This is a crucial question. A prominent Evangelical scholar and theologian, Marvin Wilson, has observed that had the Christian faithful of Germany truly understood the Jewish roots of their faith, the Holocaust would not have been possible.

A famous seminary professor would regularly inform his class, "The first thing you must do to be a good Christian is to kill the Jew inside of you." On one of those occasions, a student raised her hand and responded, "Do you mean Jesus?"

For Christians, the faith *of* Jesus strengthens and supports faith *in* Jesus, which is only as true as the faith *of* Jesus.

It is actually difficult to be against the Jewish people and their faith when you truly understand that the founder of your faith was Jewish. Harboring hatred in the Christian heart against Israel is tantamount to hating the founder of Christian faith and practice. The historical Jesus was loyal to his people and their faith, and faith *in* Jesus cannot cancel and replace the faith *of* Jesus.

The historical fact that Jesus was Jewish undermines Christian anti-Semitism. Not only was Jesus a Jew, but he upheld all the teachings of the Torah and the prophets, which embrace the eternal covenants made with the Jewish people. The close connection between Jesus and the ethical monotheism of the Jewish faith throughout history was observed by Pope John Paul when in 1986, he declared, "Whoever meets Jesus meets Judaism."

Rabbi Abraham Joshua Heschel, Professor, Jewish Theological Seminary of America

Concerning the Church's roots in faith and practice, Rabbi Abraham Joshua Heschel noted, "The vital issue in the church is to decide whether to look for its roots in Judaism and consider itself an extension of Judaism, or to look for its roots in Hellenism and consider itself as an anti-thesis to Judaism."

The Hellenistic approach to Christianity as an anti-thesis to Judaism lies at the heart of Christian anti-Semitism. In reality, it is through the Church, that Jesus brings Judaism and its ethical monotheism to the peoples of the world. For Christians, the faith *of* Jesus strengthens and supports faith *in* Jesus, and faith *in* Jesus is only as true as the faith *of* Jesus.

Consequences of the Rejection of Christianity's Jewish Roots

Today many within the Church repudiate the historical connection between a Jewish Jesus, Israel and Christian faith. One example of this is found in liberation theology, in which the Jewish people are viewed as recent colonizers of their own historic land when, in truth, Jews have always lived in the land and demonstrated deep connections to their national home.

One consequence of the denial of truth manifests in the claim that Jesus was not Jewish, but was Palestinian. The denial of a Jewish Jesus is accompanied by the allegation that the Jews killed Jesus. The Rev. Jeremiah Wright of the Church of Christ in Chicago – liberation theologian and President Obama's former pastor – has proclaimed that "Jesus was a Palestinian," and "...the Jews killed my Jesus." Similar teachings come from Bethlehem Bible College's Christ at the Checkpoint conference to this day.

The accusation that Jews killed the Palestinian Jesus raises an important question: Is this type of false preaching and teaching responsible for the death of the historical Jesus? It seems so, because this false claim contradicts history, the Bible, Nostra Aetate, many mainline denominational declarations, and Evangelical theology.

Rev. Jeremiah Wright, Pastor, Christ Church, Chicago

According to the Gospels, the Roman governor Pilate was the one who pronounced Jesus' death sentence and it was Roman soldiers who crucified Jesus. This is the historical account found in the Gospel texts. Moreover, in Christian theology, the death of Jesus is believed to be a fulfillment of Bible prophecy that brought healing and salvation to a suffering world. Divine love and human need made it imperative that Jesus die.

Nevertheless, throughout church history, in contradiction to the biblical account, Jews have been persecuted for the alleged crime of deicide, and Jewish people of all time are blamed for the death of Jesus. But, as one Jewish schoolgirl explained to her Christian classmates who accused her of killing Jesus, "I was not there. I never knew Jesus. I did not kill Christ."

A second consequence of the rejection of Christianity's Jewish roots is the fact that the proclamation of Jesus' death has sometimes been used to marginalize the living Jesus. As a result, a lawless teaching of grace has trivialized Jesus' teachings from the Sermon on the Mount and Gospel parables – teachings that demand moral action and ethical conduct.

Christians must never kill the living Jesus by the death of Jesus. The forgiveness of sins is not an excuse to avoid the Hebrew heritage of ethical monotheism in Jesus' proclamation of the kingdom. Dietrich Bonhoeffer had it right when he declared, "Cheap grace is the deadly enemy of the Church."

Indeed, consideration of the Jewish roots of Christianity demands an honest evaluation of the land of Israel, the people of Israel, and the faith of Israel found in the teachings of Jesus and the Apostle Paul. The doctrine of cheap grace can never replace covenant and conduct.

The reality is that, despite foreign colonizers from the Romans to the British, Jews have always lived in the land, and those in exile have always professed the desire to return to their national home.

A third consequence of repudiating the Jewish roots of Christianity is the fact that the Jewish people are now accused of stealing and colonizing their own homeland. The reality is that, despite foreign colonizers from the Romans to the British, Jews have always lived in the land, and those in exile have always professed the desire to return to their national home. And since 1948, they have created a democratic state in which Christian and Muslim minorities share in their governance, as demonstrated by, in just one example of many, the ability of an Arab Christian to serve as a justice on the State of Israel's Supreme Court.

Three Aspects of the Jewish Roots of Christianity

I want to examine three essential aspects of the Jewish roots of Christianity. These are the teachings of Jesus as revealed in the Gospels, the message of the Apostle Paul found in the letters he wrote to Christian communities of faith, and the question of replacement theology in relation to Israel in the Bible.

Part 1: The Teachings of Jesus

Jesus was asked which commandment was foremost of all the commandments in the Bible (Mark 12:29). He answered with the *Shema*, "Hear O Israel, the LORD our God the LORD is one" (Deut. 6:4). He also quoted the two love commandments that summarize the whole Torah. First, an individual must love God with everything in his or her heart. Second, a person must love and esteem every other human being like oneself. These two commandments summarize all the guidelines of the Scriptures that deal with the relationship between an individual and the Creator, as well as the moral code of conduct in relation to how people treat one another.

Monotheism – the recognition of the one true God of Israel – is the foundation for walking humbly with the Almighty and treating others with humane respect and dignity. The essence of Judaism is ethical monotheism and Jesus brought this teaching to the world through the growth and development of Christian discipleship through the ages. The ethical values of Judaism are taught through Jesus' interpretation of Torah in the Sermon on the Mount.

This ethical monotheism is seen in the humanitarianism of Jews and Christians dedicated to their faith traditions. In the same way that Jesus proclaimed the kingdom, the sages of ancient Israel connected the understanding of God and the commandments to receiving the sovereignty of God in daily living. Whoever prays the *Shema*, receives the kingdom.

Hear O Israel
the LORD our God
the LORD is one

The Shema

Within the Jewish community, the highly esteemed leader, Rabbi Jacob Emden, echoes this fact when he says, "Jesus brought a double goodness to the world. On the one hand he strengthened the Torah of Moses majestically... and not one of our sages spoke out more emphatically about the immutability of the Torah. On the other hand he removed idols from the nations..."

Jesus and Torah Interpretation

Before the spread of Christianity removed idols from the nations and promoted ethical conduct based on the Bible, the historical Jesus was interacting with scholars of religious law on the highest level of learning. He was obviously at home in the synagogue, and appeared to be more concerned about how to apply Torah in practice than about how to explain abstract theology. For Jesus, doing the right thing seems more important than having a perfect theology.

In the Gospels, Jesus is presented as a leader pre-eminently expert in matters of Bible interpretation and application of Oral Torah principles, and is portrayed more like a rabbi interacting with rabbis than a Christian proving that Judaism is wrong. Jesus never became a Christian.

Jesus did not cancel the words of Torah. He upheld the authentic meaning through interpretation.

However, later generations of Christians did not understand the dynamic of Jewish interpretation and application of Torah learning, and did not understand that the Jewish Jesus of the Gospels debated issues of Torah observance. Indeed, he declared, "Do not think that I have come to abolish the Law or the Prophets; I did not come to abolish but to fulfill" (Matt 5:17).

Jesus gives deeper spiritual meaning and practical application to the Ten Commandments through a fresh interpretation of Torah. Jesus did not cancel the words of Torah. His declaration means that he accepted the Torah completely. He upheld the authentic meaning through interpretation. The Sermon on the Mount is an intensification of the Torah, in which Jesus' message in no way compromises or abolishes the words of the sacred text. In fact, he made it clear that not one jot or letter could be canceled from the Torah.

The ancient rabbis interpreted the deeper meaning of the Torah for practical application in a similar way. The early Tannaitic teacher, Rabbi Simeon bar Yochai, gave the example of King Solomon who tried to cancel a letter of the Torah through a creative interpretation.

Notwithstanding his legendary wisdom, King Solomon was known for his many wives, his fabulous stables with impressive horses, and his immense wealth. He lived like this in spite of the fact the Torah explicitly commands that the king must not "multiply to himself" wives, horses, or gold (Deut 17:16-17). But Solomon attempted to change the entire meaning of the commandment by getting rid of the smallest Hebrew letter, *yod* from the verb in this command.

Without the tiny letter *yod*, the commandment prohibiting the king of Israel from multiplying wives, horses, and money could be completely reinterpreted to be an imperative verb. King Solomon read the negative word lo as a dative of advantage. Therefore, Solomon could interpret this text as saying that the king is commanded to, "multiply for himself" wives, horses, together with silver and gold.

The Hebrew Letter "Yod"

In the Jerusalem Talmud, Rabbi Simeon explains how the tiny letter, which had been abolished from the Torah, complained to the Almighty. The divine response is very strong, "Solomon and a thousand like him will be canceled, but not one tiny letter will be abolished from the Torah." This episode is instructive in relation to the Sermon on the Mount even though the Jerusalem Talmud was written in the first quarter of the second century when Rabbi Simeon was one of the five disciples of Rabbi Akiva. Jesus made it clear that not one jot or tittle could be removed from Torah, and the Talmud prohibits the removal of a letter or re-interpretation of Torah as well.

Proper interpretation of Torah gives a more profound application. In fact, Jesus' application of "Do not kill" and "Do not commit adultery" made Torah observance more difficult. As a Jewish teacher from Second Temple Period Judaism, Jesus is quite stringent when he teaches that anger leads to murder and lust in the heart leads to adultery. He intensifies the authentic meaning of Torah through insightful application. The Christian notion that Jesus canceled Torah is misguided and disconnected from the Jewish roots of the first century faith experience.

Jesus and Sabbath Observance

Jesus observed the Jewish Sabbath. When issues relating to Sabbath observance were raised, Jesus answered questions by explaining the Oral Torah and defending his approach to Jewish law. For example, Jesus argued that healing on the Sabbath was permitted because saving life overrides the ritual observance connected to the sanctity of the day. The Pharisees would have found his arguments based upon the Oral Torah very sound and all Rabbis today would agree.

Other influential religious movements of the time like the Sadducees and the Essenes may well have disagreed. The Sadducees were biblical literalists and rejected the Oral Torah, which made practical application of the written sacred word. That they were opposed to the teachings of Jesus is demonstrated by the fact that they played a prominent role together with the Roman authorities in the events of the last week of Jesus' life.

Jesus answered questions by explaining the Oral Torah and defending his approach to Jewish law.

The Essenes – the producers of the Dead Sea Scrolls – were also very strict in their interpretation of the written word. The Dead Sea Community was much more strict in legal enactments and they complained about the lenient rulings of the Pharisees by referring to them as the "ones seeking after the smooth matters."

The Damascus Covenant, a document first discovered in the Cairo Geniza and then discovered among the Dead Sea Scrolls, demonstrated a radical approach to the observance of the Sabbath. This text is similar to the perspective of the Essenes and could likely represent some views of the Sadducees as well. It teaches that if your ox falls into a pit on the Sabbath, you must by no means lift it out.

On the other hand, the Talmud, which may well represent the results of earlier discussion and debate by the Pharisees, teaches that if your cow falls into a pit on the Sabbath you are permitted to provide cushions for comfort. If the animal climbs out, he climbs out. It would seem that for the Pharisees, it was permitted to lift an ox out of the ditch on the Sabbath.

Dead Sea Scrolls in the Shrine of the Book, Israel Museum, Jerusalem

When Jesus made a similar halakhic argument in the synagogue, it is likely his audience was made up of Pharisees or those closely connected to their views of Oral Torah, including the permissibility of lifting an ox out of the ditch on the Sabbath. Based upon the Oral Torah, he argued that healing is permitted on Shabbat because if your ox falls into a pit on Shabbat you are expected to alleviate the suffering of the animal and lift it out. In fact, the rescue of an animal in pain is required on the Sabbath on the basis of saving life.

The four Gospels of the Christian Scriptures all record clear references to halakhah in Jesus' arguments when he stated that he and his disciples keep the Sabbath. While groups such as the Sadducees and the Essenes would not have agreed, many, if not the vast majority, of Pharisees would likely have found the arguments presented by Jesus quite compelling. In fact, the Pharisees and the rabbis after them placed immense significance upon the value of life, and ruled that the saving of life overrides the Sabbath law.

In an early Tannaitic commentary on the Book of Exodus, the rabbis discussed the importance of saving life. In the discussion presented in this text, Rabbi Simeon ben Menasyah interpreted Exodus 31:13, where it says, the Sabbath "is holy unto you" as meaning, "The Sabbath is given over to you but you are not given over to the Sabbath." Similarly, Jesus taught, "The Sabbath was made for man, not man for the Sabbath" (Mark 2:27).

The Jewishness of Jesus is most certainly revealed through his teachings on the observance of the Sabbath.

In Genesis, the final act of Creation was the creation of the human being. First God prepared a beautiful world full of blessing to be enjoyed by humankind, and then humans were created on the eve of Sabbath to enter into the time of rest with the Creator. So literally, as Rabbi Simeon and Jesus taught, the Sabbath was made for man as an experience of joy and blessing. The Jewishness of Jesus is most certainly revealed through his teachings on the observance of the Sabbath and in the way he made direct reference to the Oral Torah.

Jesus and the Pharisees

It must be recognized that although Jesus criticized the hypocritical practices of some Pharisees, he did not condemn their teachings. In fact, Jesus upheld the teachings of the scribes and Pharisees regarding the Oral Torah. On the one hand, Jesus had sharp criticism for those who preach but do not practice. But on the other hand he declared, "so practice and observe whatever they tell you..." (Matt 23:3).

The Talmud also has harsh criticism for the hypocritical practices of some Pharisees. Likewise, Catholics criticize hypocritical Catholics and Baptists criticize Baptists. Jesus' criticism of the Pharisees demonstrates that he was actually very close to the Pharisees in theology and teachings relating to the interpretation and practical application of Scripture.

The Talmud lists seven types of Pharisees. The types are remarkably similar to the criticisms given by Jesus, such as his critique of the "shoulder Pharisee." This type of hypocrite binds heavy burdens upon the shoulders of others to carry but fails to practice his own teachings. Both Jesus and the rabbis criticize this type of spiritual leader.

Jesus was fiercely loyal to his people and firmly upheld Torah teachings.

However, there is also a positive type of Pharisee mentioned in the Talmud – the Pharisee of love. This Pharisee is compared to Abraham and is highly esteemed in the teaching of the rabbis who were connected to the Pharisees and their interpretation of the written Torah. Likewise, Jesus praised the one who shows compassion to others as the "Pharisee of love." In proclaiming the kingdom message, Jesus was fiercely loyal to his people and firmly upheld Torah teachings. Without any doubt, the Jesus portrayed in the Gospels is totally Jewish.

Part 2: The Apostle Paul and His Message

The Apostle Paul is perhaps the Pharisee we know the most about because of the preservation of his own writings in the Christian Testament. He clearly describes himself as a Pharisee and he is proud of his heritage. In fact, he presents himself as a Pharisee of Pharisees and therefore, he must be studied as a first century example of the movement. He wrote letters to communities of faith, many of which he helped to establish. The authorship of many of these letters is undisputed even by the most critical of scholars, and some scholars have observed that through his writings, we have direct access to the thoughts and teachings of an historical Pharisee.

I would like to make a connection between the "Pharisee of love" compared to Abraham in the Talmud, and the emphasis in the writings of the Apostle Paul on love and the faith of Abraham. But first, some background on how the Talmudic literature portrays seven types of Pharisees, six of which are most likely negative characterizations.

Clearly the themes of love for God and others, and practicing what is preached, were dear to the Pharisee in both the Talmud and in the writings of Paul.

The Talmudic depictions show a type of Pharisee who teaches but does not practice what is being taught. Jesus taught that the scribes and Pharisees sit on the seat of Moses and that their teachings are full of wisdom that should be followed. In Matthew 23:2, he declared, "Do what they say..." However Jesus also criticized the hypocritical behavior of some Pharisees who preached well, but did not practice what they preach. This same criticism is found in the Talmud where personal conduct that mirrors ethical teaching is promoted.

Sadly sometimes, Christianity has characterized the teachings of the Pharisees as evil without learning their message from the best sources. While six types of Pharisees are most likely examples of inferior conduct, the seventh type of Pharisee is to be praised and emulated. Abraham represents this type and he is portrayed as the "Pharisee of love", whose conduct demonstrated love for God and love for others through his faith experience.

The Apostle Paul

The Apostle Paul seems to replicate the Talmudic teachings when he talks about the faith of Abraham in his epistle to the Romans and the pre-eminent message of love in 1 Corinthians 13. The concluding verse of this love chapter, "These three remain forever, faith, hope, and love – but the greatest of these is love," is rooted in the foundation of the Pharisaic interpretation of Holy Scripture. In the rabbinic portrayal of our father Abraham, this man of faith opened wide his tent to share with others the message of God's love.

Clearly the themes of love for God and others, and practicing what is preached, were dear to the Pharisee in both the Talmud and in the writings of Paul.

Paul's Audience

Jesus declared, "I was sent only to the lost sheep of the House of Israel" (Matt 15:24). This declaration demonstrates Jesus' awareness of his Jewish background and the focus of his career. Paul, on the other hand, was sent to the non-Jewish world and was writing to non-Jewish readers who had abandoned the paganism and idolatry of the surrounding culture and had embraced faith in the one true God of Israel through the Jew, Jesus of Nazareth.

Through his writings, it is apparent that Paul longed to see the vision of the Hebrew prophets realized. The prophets envisioned a future where the pagan non-Jewish world would reject idolatry and pray to the God of Abraham, Isaac, and Jacob alongside the Jewish people. They declare that Israel is to be a light for the teachings of Torah to go forth from Zion to the entire world. Therefore, the Temple must be a house of prayer for all peoples.

Paul on the Relationship of Christians to Israel and the Jewish People

The fact that Paul was writing to non-Jewish readers provides insight into what he had to say about the future of Israel and how Christians are related to Israel and the Jewish people. Without understanding the context in which he wrote, Paul's message of engraftment found in Romans 9-11 – that non-Jewish heathens would be engrafted into Israel like a twig to a tree – is misunderstood. As a result, Paul's view of the relationship of Christians to Israel and the Jewish people is very different than the one adopted later in some church teachings.

The gifts and callings of God to Israel can never be revoked. (Rom 11:20)

In his letter to the Romans, Paul was writing to the community of faith in Rome, the capital of the Roman Empire. This community of largely non-Jewish believers had experienced significant upheaval. Jews had been expelled from Rome by the authorities, and then been allowed to return. As a result, social tensions developed quite naturally between those who had been expelled and those who had not. Paul wrote this letter to tackle complex issues that arose and made chapters 9, 10, and 11 the core message of his presentation.

In these chapters, he first made it clear that the gifts and callings of God to Israel can never be revoked (Rom 11:20). Second, he defined Israel as including Jewish people who continued in their faith tradition without receiving Jesus (Rom 9:1-5). Their "no" to Jesus was their "yes" to God and the Bible, and the fact that they remained faithful to their beliefs had opened the opportunity for non-Jews to come into a faith experience through Jesus.

Paul rejected the idea that the preaching of faith canceled the Torah and its promises to the Jews. (Rom 3:31)

This text does not indicate that Paul in any way embraced the idea that the physical children of Abraham, Isaac, and Jacob had been replaced or disinherited by those who came to faith in Jesus. For him the divine strategy of redemption was being implemented through Israel and the Church. Likely one of the main reasons or even the primary purpose of writing the letter was to dispel forever and always the notion that God had rejected the Jewish people. Indeed, Paul rejected the idea that the preaching of faith canceled the Torah and its promises to the Jews (Rom 3:31).

As highly revered Christian theologian Karl Barth explained, "Without any doubt the Jews are to this very day the chosen people of God in the same sense as they have been so from the beginning, according to the Old and New Testaments. They have the promise of God and if we Christians from among the Gentiles have it too, then it is only as those chosen with them; as guest in their house, as new wood grafted onto their old tree." Here Barth is saying again what the Apostle Paul states in Romans 9-11 so clearly, that it is the root that nourishes the branch, and the eternal covenant promised to the people of Israel can never be compromised.

Rev. Karl Barth

Unfortunately, however, throughout history, the Church has claimed that the tree of Israel was cut down and replaced, that Israel is no more and now the true Israel is the Church. As a result, many Christians read the Bible as if they have replaced Israel, and as if the Jewish people are erased from history. They recast themselves into the promises made to the physical descendants of Abraham and replace Israel with the Church.

Apparently this concept of replacement had already sprouted when Paul wrote his letter to the

Romans, because he felt the need to teach that it is the root, which is Israel, that nourishes the branch, which is the Church.

Part 3: Replacement Theology and Israel in the Bible

Replacement theology teaches that the covenants and callings upon Israel detailed in the Hebrew Bible have been canceled and replaced by the covenant with the Church found in the Christian Scriptures. The chosen Church has supplanted the Jewish people as the "true Israel." Historical Israel is redefined as spiritual Israel through theological re-interpretation of eternal covenantal promises. As a result, the eternal covenant with Israel is no longer valid because Israel has been replaced by the Church.

In contrast to replacement theology, Jesus upheld the immutability of the Older Testament and the Apostle Paul declared that the gifts and callings for Israel are irrevocable and divinely appointed. Therefore, a Christian theology concerning Israel that embraces engraftment and fulfillment of divine covenant and promise is much more aligned with the teachings of Jesus and Paul than a replacement theology that denies the faith of Jesus while proclaiming a perverted claim for exclusivity.

Paul's teaching is consistent with the Hebrew Scriptures, which view Israel as the physical descendants of Abraham, Isaac, and Jacob.

Indeed, the Apostle Paul did not refer to Israel as something past, but used the present tense when he wrote, "They are Israelites and to them belong the sonship, the glory, the covenants, the giving of the law, the worship, and the promises, and of their race, according to the flesh, is the Christ" (Rom 9:4-5). These words alone forever refute the teaching of replacement theology because the apostle never claimed that they used to be Israelites and have now been replaced by others.

Paul's teaching is consistent with the Hebrew Scriptures, which view Israel as the physical descendants of Abraham, Isaac, and Jacob. Israel is mentioned some 2,400 times in the Older Testament with this family connection, which means that the family of Israel is forever connected to their faith experience, their covenantal land, and the practice of their religious heritage. Israel is also mentioned nearly 80 times in the Christian Testament with the same meaning, and this testament does not redefine Israel. Indeed, the land, the people, and the faith cannot be separated, as they are inter-connected throughout the Jewish and Christian Bible.

Commonalities of Jewish and Christian Faith

Evangelical Bible-believing-Christians share many commonalities with the Jewish community of faith. The Scriptures that Jews and Christians have in common draw them together in a common purpose. Both Jewish and Christian communities of faith emphasize loving God with all your heart and loving your neighbor as yourself. Leading historic rabbis like esteemed community leader and teacher Jacob Emden from the 18th century observed that Christianity taught ethical monotheism based upon the message of Jesus. As a result, he believed that Christianity served the common good.

Without disregarding the differences between Judaism and Christianity, which are profound and distinctive, the common bond of loving God and neighbor in ethical monotheism is a strong and important connection.

Jewish and Christian communities study the Bible and share a faith in the promises of the Torah and the prophets for the Jewish people. The Hebrew prophets longed for all the peoples of the world to come to faith in God and to live a life based upon the ethical teachings of their Bible. Without disregarding the differences between Judaism and Christianity, which are profound and distinctive, the common bond of loving God and neighbor in ethical monotheism is a strong and important connection.

On this day when we remember Rev. Dr. Martin Luther King, it is important to recall his strong support for the modern state of Israel. Rev. Dr. King was first a Baptist preacher and strong evangelical leader. His faith strengthened him in his fight for social justice and equality. Moreover, he believed strongly in establishing and protecting Israel. He was certainly a Christian Zionist. Speaking to the annual convention of the Rabbinic Assembly on March 25, 1968, he declared:

> Peace for Israel means security, and we must stand with all of our might to protect its right to exist, its territorial integrity. I see Israel, and never mind saying it, as one of the great outposts of democracy in the world, and a marvelous example of what can be done, how desert land almost can be transformed into an oasis of brotherhood and democracy. Peace for Israel means security and that security must be a reality.

It should be noted that Rabbi Dr. Abraham Joshua Heschel became a close friend of Dr. King and participated in the historic Selma march. Rabbi Dr. Heschel commented that he felt like his feet were praying as he marched for equality and justice on that hot summer day. On Rabbi Dr. Heschel's 60th birthday, Rev. Dr. King was invited to come and address 800 rabbis who had come to honor Rabbi Dr. Heschel. The rabbis had learned to sing, "We shall overcome" in Hebrew and greeted their guest speaker singing the familiar tune with Hebrew words, *Anu Nitgaber*.

Rev. Dr. Martin Luther King

In conclusion, the current agenda that intends to transform evangelical Christian faith and practice in relation to Israel is nothing more than a revived version of anti-Semitism, anti-Zionism, and replacement theology that challenges Israel's right to exist within secure and recognized borders.

The proponents of this calculated move within evangelical Christianity to disengage from Scriptural teachings that uphold the eternal covenantal relationship between God and the Jewish people need to answer the question: Does the State of Israel have a right to exist? When the connection between a Jewish Jesus, Israel and Christian faith as demonstrated through the teachings of Jesus and the Apostle Paul are considered in their biblical and historical context, the only possible answer to this question is: Yes.

Jewish-Christian Relations and Cooperation for Israel

Rabbi Yitzchok Adlerstein

Rabbi Yitzchok Adlerstein is an Orthodox rabbi who has played an important role as spokesman, teacher, and writer on behalf of Orthodox Judaism. He is also the director of Interfaith Affairs for the Simon Wiesenthal Center. As an accomplished scholar and seasoned veteran in interfaith dialogue, Rabbi Adlerstein brings an essential perspective to the subject of Jewish-Christian cooperation in support of Israel.

Why should Jews and Christians work together for the benefit of the State of Israel? There are two distinct reasons and the difference between them is crucial. One is for the sake of justice. And the other reason is religious.

Justice Reasons

In the beginning of the Book of Exodus, Moses goes out and sees an Egyptian taskmaster beating a Jewish slave. He intervenes, takes matters into his own hands, and kills the Egyptian.

Moses was just as eager and quick to react to save someone else from a miscarriage of justice as he was to act on behalf of one of his own brothers.

In the following narrative, Moses arrives in the land of Midian, a stranger in a xenophobic territory. He sees a group of young women in distress and intervenes by rescuing the women.

Why are these two narratives juxtaposed?

One of the great teachers of the early twentieth century, Rabbi Yerucham, explains that the second narrative is crucial to our understanding of the first. Don't think that Moses was compelled to act because of nationalistic fervor on his part. Don't make the mistake of thinking that Moses acted just because he could not bear to see his own people so mistreated. G-d wants you to know that Moses was just as eager and quick to react to save someone else from a miscarriage of justice as he was to act on behalf of one of his own brothers.

Maimonides, the great philosopher of the Middle Ages, wrote in his *Guide for the Perplexed* that this is how G-d chooses his prophets. He looks for someone with an oversized sense of justice, someone who will rise to the occasion whenever they see a miscarriage of justice. I've met several people like that. For example, Dexter Van Zile of CAMERA.

Dexter comes from a historic mainline church. He looked around one day and said, "You know this just doesn't make sense. My ancestors came over on the Mayflower, and risked their lives to start a new lifestyle that offered religious liberty and tolerance for everyone. To think that my church was now beating up on Israel was more than I could take." There is nothing in it for Dexter other than the perception that an injustice was being done.

Maimonides

Justice demands that people recognize that Israel is the only democratic state in the Middle East, the only one where Christians are safe, where Christianity is growing, where women and gays do not have to fear for their lives.

I work with a group of Presbyterians who, for different reasons than Evangelicals, support Israel and work tirelessly on its behalf. If you ask any of them, it's not because of a promise in Genesis. It's because, as Christians, they are incensed by the constant injustice in the treatment of Israel – in the press, in academia and in international forums.

Justice demands that people recognize that Israel is the only democratic state in the Middle East, the only one where Christians are safe, where Christianity is growing, where women and gays do not have to fear for their lives. So why is this country – one that has and continues to offer the world so much – targeted by so many churches as the *only* object of their venom?

There is a gross injustice being done and those who are interested in justice should be working on the same team to correct that injustice. Israel may not be a perfect state, but it is no more or less perfect than any other state in the world. Yet it is the only one that is the focus of so much animus and contempt. And, it is the only state whose right to self-determination in its own country is rejected by so many in the world.

Behind this injustice are two themes that affect Jews and Christians alike – anti-Semitism and a far-left agenda.

Anti-Semitism lies behind the extreme hatred of Israel. Such hatred never stops with Jews alone. It always morphs into contempt and loathing for other groups, as well. Jews and Christians must work to combat anti-Semitism and realize that this is what fuels much of the anti-Israel activity.

The far-left agenda would have us naively erase all notions of nationhood, of borders, of private property, of power, of authority, and all distinctions between people. Unfortunately, contempt from the left does not end with Israel as a so-called "colonialist" entity. It extends to the United States as well, because the U.S. is powerful and successful.

Religious Reasons

There are significant numbers of Christian supporters of Israel – usually conservative Christians – who respond to Israel for reasons other than, or in addition to, issues of justice. Some of them are Evangelicals and Pentecostals, who make up the single fastest growing segment of Christendom in many parts of the world.

Without minimizing the number of theological differences between believing Jews and Evangelicals, the extent of shared values is staggering. Given that these shared values are now threatened in a radically changing society, a new partnership and alliance between believing Christians and believing Jews is essential for self-preservation. Belief in, and support of, the State of Israel is often the glue that brings us together.

We have a shared belief in a G-d who creates, a G-d who cares about humankind and individual people, who legislates morality and law, and who assigns limits to human behavior, personal and political. This can be reduced to two words: Bible and Law, a common belief in the power of the Bible and seeing it as the will of G-d.

Among Christian Zionists, there are two potent groups. The first represents premillenial dispensationalists – for example, Christians United For Israel (CUFI), whom I greatly admire and support. However, CUFI does not represent the theological position of most Evangelicals, and the State of Israel cannot afford to miss the other 60 or more percent of Evangelicals who support Israel for other reasons.

I believe that G-d does have a special covenant with the Jewish people. But he has a glorious game plan for mankind as well.

The second group of Christian Zionists looks at the rebirth of the country, of a nation, as a fulfillment of G-d's covenant to the Jewish people, which they value as one of several covenants that G-d made. The belief in the efficacy of the covenant is often not attached to any particular biblical prophecy for the future, which they may actually argue against from a theological point of view.

I believe that G-d does have a special covenant with the Jewish people. But he has a glorious game plan for mankind as well. When you witness G-d maintaining his covenant with the Jewish people, it offers support for the idea that G-d will always be with all of mankind.

Working Together to Face the Challenges Before Us

Coming together on Israel is only part of what we agree upon. The larger issue is what is happening within our society. Jews and Christians who are brought together in appreciation of the great State of Israel can also work together for a better America and a better world in which the honor and glory of G-d are allowed to shine again among people. I'm convinced that the majority of American people believe strongly in the Word of G-d, but they need reminding from time to time. And that is where Jews and Christians can help each other.

So, as religious Christians and Jews, we must articulate the justice reasons for why we support Israel because our young people are focused on justice, whether they are in Evangelical churches, Jewish synagogues, or neither.

We are faced with the challenge of addressing a new generation that has only seen Israel through the eyes of a hostile media. This generation never saw the Israel that was the David. They see it only as the Goliath, and many have been only too eager to play on this new Goliath image.

In today's world, Israel has a difficult time basing its existence or legitimacy on the Bible alone. As a believing Jew, I have no problem doing that myself. But the world won't necessarily buy the idea of an Israel that is legitimate because G-d said so. Too many people do not believe this to be the case, and some don't even believe in G-d in the first place.

So, as religious Christians and Jews, we must articulate the justice reasons for why we support Israel because our young people are focused on justice, whether they are in Evangelical churches, Jewish synagogues, or neither.

In addition, we must be able to work together to see the big picture, what is happening to society, and then get together and pool our resources to keep young people involved in religion.

Too often, we speak old speak. We use old techniques; we use old marketing. We are not using social media and You-Tube as effectively as we should. Things have changed. People don't read anymore. So, we must present G-d in terms that people, young people in particular, can relate to. And we need to do this work together.

In order to create a very different relationship with the Christian world, Jews must cut through the hostility of 2000 years of negative Christian-Jewish relations. Despite the history of relations in the past and during the Holocaust, we must remind skeptics of the positive stories about Christians who risked their lives in the Holocaust to save Jews. We must remind them about those children of anti-Semites who are now the greatest philo-Semites.

We must demonstrate a new paradigm of understanding and bridge-building, and we must be able to accept the grace of our friends from outside the Jewish community, especially when it comes from a great place meant to serve the honor of G-d.

A Reason for Hope: Christians United for Israel

Randal Neal

Randal Neal is the Western Regional Coordinator for Christians United for Israel. He speaks throughout thirteen western states on topics concerning Israel and Christian support for the Jewish State. He pioneered the programming and procedures that have been implemented nationally to grow CUFI into the largest pro-Israel organization in America, and is among the most sought after Christian speakers on the history of Christian anti-Semitism and the Biblical mandate to support Israel.

Editor's Introduction

The purpose of Christians United For Israel (CUFI) is to provide a national association through which every pro-Israel church, para-church organization, ministry or individual in America can speak and act with one voice in support of Israel in matters related to Biblical issues.

Founded in 2006, CUFI has more than 3 million members, spanning all fifty states, as of Summer 2016.

Since its inception, CUFI has held more than 2,500 pro-Israel events in cities and towns across the country, including more than 300 Nights to Honor Israel. The organization presently holds an average of 30 pro-Israel events each month and hosts an annual summit in Washington DC every July for the purpose of educating thousands of attendees about current events, and equipping them to lobby elected officials on Capital Hill.

Throughout the year, CUFI sends out action alerts to enable its members to contact their members of Congress or the Administration on critical policy issues.

During the conference, Randal Neal gave a brief presentation about CUFI, which included a short video.

Highlights from his talk are as follows:

Our purpose is to send a message of solidarity with Jews, and to send a message to Christians that they are ambassadors for the Jewish people and the Jewish State.

February 6th [2016] will mark the tenth anniversary of the birth of CUFI, when 412 Christians met in San Antonio, TX to hear the vision for an organization that would be by design, without exception, non-conversionary to the Jewish people.

Today, we have over 3 million members and are by far the largest pro-Israel organization in the world. What is happening through CUFI is a move of God. It's not simply the plan or the orchestration of an organization.

Our purpose is to send a message of solidarity with Jews, and to send a message to Christians that they are ambassadors for the Jewish people and the Jewish State. Christians must be aware of 1700 years of horrific history – not to rewrite it, not to self-loathe for it, but to commit to change the trend so that our history does not repeat itself. That is what CUFI endeavors to do.

I would like to explain how I got involved as an activist for Israel. I was in a men's Bible study years ago, and I asked the members: "This Israel [in the Bible], is this the Israel on CNN?" And they said to me: "No, whenever you see Israel [in the Bible], just pretend it says the church there."

Our purpose is to mobilize the complacent, and to inoculate attendees against a deceptive, anti-Israel message being used to erode Evangelical support for the Jewish State.

That is how I was introduced to replacement theology. I obviously didn't hook my wagon to that, or I wouldn't be here right now. That interaction is what caused me to start watching and paying attention, and since that time, I have developed workshops and presentations refuting replacement and supersessionist theologies.

Another step on the path that led me to what I am doing today came when an AIPAC leader said to me: "Great, you love Israel. What are you doing for Israel?" In addition to challenging me, she gave me CAMERA magazines to read.

Before reading the material from CAMERA, I didn't really believe in media bias – that sounded like conspiracy theory to me. But during the years of the Oslo Accords, I saw an article with the headline, "Israel Attacks Muslim Holy Sites." That headline made the hair on my neck stand on end, and that was when I decided to get involved in political activism for Israel.

Let me describe what CUFI does. Every single month, we host an average of 30 pro-Israel events in churches across the nation. Our purpose is to mobilize the complacent, and to inoculate attendees against a deceptive, anti-Israel message being used to erode Evangelical support for the Jewish State. One of our most important activities is CUFI on Campus. There are some 150 chapters on campuses across this country. The students receive intense training to deal with BDS (Boycott, Divestment and Sanctions against Israel) and to debate on behalf of Israel on campus.

Our flagship event is our Washington DC Summit, which takes place annually. Every July, we bring about 5000 Christians to Capitol Hill to send the message that not only Jewish organizations, but Christian ones too, want Congress to support strong US-Israel relations. The first year, they didn't know we were coming, the second year, they hoped we wouldn't come back, the third year, they realized we weren't going away, and now we have their attention.

We are releasing our first book, "Israel for Critical Thinkers." Our first documentary is "Looking Through the Looking Glass," and our first weekly television program on TBN is being launched with Eric Stakelback. We continue to do what we can to dig in a little bit deeper.

I'm here to give you encouragement, and show our Jewish partners that there are millions of agents in the goyim underground who are trying to do everything we can to turn the tide.

Appendices

Empowered 21 and Christians Who Promote Anti-Israel Propaganda

Tricia Miller, Ph.D.

This article was originally published in Breaking Israel News on July 9, 2015.

Empowered21 (E21), a worldwide Christian organization based in Tulsa, OK and the sponsor of a Global Congress in Jerusalem in May 2015, may be endangering its credibility, and the credibility of the Christian faith it seeks to propagate, because of its relationship with Palestinian Christians who promote a fallacious anti-Israel narrative.

This global entity, which intends to "shape the future of the Spirit-empowered movement" and evangelize every person on earth by 2033, claims to represent 640,000,000 Evangelical and pentecostal Christians. Therefore, the potential fallout from an alliance with those who spread dishonest propaganda against Israel is significant.

At the recent conference, E21 co-chair Billy Wilson and others repeatedly emphasized the necessity of Christian unity for the purpose of "world evangelization in our generation." The problem with this call to unity stems from E21's unreflective support for, and involvement with, Palestinian Christian leaders who promote a narrative rooted in demonization of Jews, delegitimization of Israel, and erroneous theology.

The problem with this call to unity stems from E21's unreflective support for, and involvement with, Palestinian Christian leaders who promote a narrative rooted in demonization of Jews, delegitimization of Israel, and erroneous theology.

This relationship is demonstrated in part, through the inclusion of Jack Sara, president of Bethlehem Bible College, as one of the leaders in E21's Global Congress. Sara's participation is particularly troubling because Bethlehem Bible College (BBC) and the Christ at the Checkpoint (CaTC) conferences it sponsors are some of the primary promoters of virulent anti-Jewish/anti-Israel propaganda.

The logo for Christ at the Checkpoint depicts a church behind the security barrier built by Israel. Through imagery and content, these conferences present a one-sided narrative that perpetuates the two millennia-old Christian doctrine that Jews are an obstacle to God's purposes. As a result, Jews are demonized, the Jewish state is delegitimized, and Christians are encouraged to accept the message in the name of peace and justice.

CaTC's anti-Jewish narrative is rooted in a customized replacement theology and a Palestinian version of liberation theology. Traditional replacement theology says that God no longer has any purpose for Israel or the Jews and that God's work on earth is now being done through Christians and the Church. This teaching promotes contempt for Jews, and has provided justification for two millennia of anti-Semitic violence.

This narrative is rooted in a customized replacement theology and a Palestinian version of liberation theology. Traditional replacement theology says that God no longer has any purpose for Israel or the Jews and that God's work on earth is now being done through Christians and the Church. This teaching promotes contempt for Jews, and has provided justification for two millennia of anti-Semitic violence.

Palestinian replacement theology rewrites history by claiming that Jesus and the first Christians were all Palestinians, and that the Palestinians – not the Jews – are the indigenous people in the land. This assertion means that the Palestinian people are the rightful owners of the land, which serves their political agenda very nicely by delegitimizing the existence of the Jewish State.

Palestinian liberation theology depicts Palestinians as victims who need to be liberated from Israeli occupation. This narrative is particularly appealing to an Evangelical audience susceptible to a message emphasizing the need for peace and justice, but has no understanding of the historical or political context of current events necessary to counter the lies and distortions supported by this theology.

The promotion of, or adherence to, any theology that is customized for the purpose of promoting a political agenda undermines the credibility of historic Christian faith.

The promotion of, or adherence to, any theology that is customized for the purpose of promoting a political agenda undermines the credibility of historic Christian faith.

Therefore, the perpetuation of 2,000-year-old anti-Jewish canards and erroneous theology by BBC and CaTC is a serious problem. Consequently, it is imperative that the leaders of E21 consider the repercussions of not distancing themselves from this demonizing narrative, even as they express the understandable desire to support their Palestinian brethren.

E21's collaboration with local Christians was further evidenced through the scheduling of a service in Manger Square in Bethlehem, before it was cancelled with one days notice due to "significant political and religious pressure." In response to this unexpected development, E21 co-chair Wilson "spent the afternoon in Manger Square trying to find a way to further support our Christian brothers in there, including considering the possibility of other alternative venues."

Wilson's intent to "support our Christian brothers in there" by scheduling a service in Bethlehem, and the involvement of the president of BBC in the leadership of E21 are consistent with the conference's emphasis on the importance of Christian unity. This would be an ideal goal in an ideal world. However, in this case, E21's cooperation with Palestinian Christian organizations that have a track record of anti-Israel activism may provide a venue through which their false narrative is promoted to a global audience.

E21's cooperation with Palestinian Christian organizations that have a track record of anti-Israel activism may provide a venue through which their false narrative is promoted to a global audience.

In light of this threat, the leadership of Empowered 21 needs to reconsider how they define their stand in "unity" with those who promote anti-Israel propaganda based on erroneous theology, demonization of Jews, and delegitimization of Israel.

Otherwise, the credibility of this global movement and the Christian faith it seeks to propagate will be compromised, and its intent to "shape the future of the Spirit-empowered movement" will be an issue of great concern.

Empowered21 Threatens Jewish-Christian Relations

Tricia Miller, Ph.D.

This article was originally published in The Times of Israel blogs on July 21, 2015.

Empowered21 (E21), a worldwide Christian organization based in Tulsa OK, is threatening Jewish-Christian relations as a result of its seemingly unreflective alliance with Palestinian Christians who propagate a narrative rooted in demonization of Jews and the Jewish State.

At its Global Congress in Jerusalem in May 2015, co-chair Billy Wilson and others placed a significant amount of emphasis on the necessity of Christian unity for the purpose of "world evangelization in our generation." This unqualified call to unity is cause for significant concern because it suggests an expectation of solidarity with E21 conference participants who are also leaders in Palestinian Christian organizations such as Bethlehem Bible College (BBC) and Christ at the Checkpoint (CaTC) Conferences – both of which are primary promoters of virulent anti-Jewish/anti-Israel propaganda.

The first problem with this account is that it is simply not true.

The relationship between E21 and those who promote such pernicious dogma is demonstrated in part, through the inclusion of Jack Sara, president of Bethlehem Bible College. Sara was scheduled to participate in a breakout session and he was also a member of the committee, "Exploring the Land of Pentecost," which was responsible for educating attendees about places they would tour during the conference.

Sara's participation is problematic because his Bible College sponsors the biannual Christ at the Checkpoint conferences in Bethlehem. The representation of a church behind the security barrier built by Israel in the logo for these events demonstrates the central role the barrier plays in the prejudiced narrative promoted through these conferences.

Another problem with Awad's statement is that it does not address the reason the barrier was built, which was to prevent terror attacks.

According to Sami Awad, executive director of the Holy Land Trust, which is a co-sponsor of CaTC:

Today Bethlehem is a city that is completely surrounded by walls and fences. The wall just completely engulfs the city. Living in the wall is like living in a big prison where you are deemed guilty and that's why you live in this prison. Every day we see the wall. It's very big and very ugly, completely surrounding us, completely engulfing us.

The first problem with this account is that it is simply not true. The security barrier does not completely surround Bethlehem. However, it does separate the city from Jerusalem, and as a result, has effectively stopped the deadly terror attacks against Israeli citizens that intensified during the Second Intifada.

Another problem with Awad's statement is that it does not address the reason the barrier was built, which was to prevent terror attacks. This is a revealing example of the one-sided story presented at CaTC in which the two millennia-old Christian allegation that Jews are an obstacle to God's purposes is perpetuated. The combination of the depictation of a church behind the barrier, and Awad's deceptive and inaccurate description of that barrier, contributes to the demonization of Jews and the Jewish state.

Christ at the Checkpoint took this demonization to a new low through the posting of a video on YouTube on March 26, 2015. The video was produced to promote a CaTC Young Adult conference in July 2015.

Empowered 21's unqualified expectation that attendees at the Global Congress stand in unity with those who proliferate material that perpetuates the demonization of Jews and the State of Israel is both alarming and destructive.

In this video, images of ISIS captives about to be beheaded are juxtapositioned with images of the security barrier Israel built to protect its citizens from suicide bombers.
Images of the Jordanian pilot about to be burned alive in a cage by ISIS are juxtapositioned with scenes of people going through a checkpoint.

And images of the ISIS flag are juxtapositioned with those of the Israeli flag.

The obvious implication is that the security measures Israel has been forced to take in response to Palestinian suicide bombers is equivalent to what ISIS is doing to people as it seeks to forcibly establish a caliphate ruled by an extreme form of Islamic law.

Empowered 21's unqualified expectation that attendees at the Global Congress stand in unity with those who proliferate material that perpetuates the demonization of Jews and the State of Israel is both alarming and destructive.

It is alarming because an unreflective alliance with Palestinian Christian leaders who promote such virulent propaganda suggests that this worldwide movement – which represents a significant part of Christendom that has historically supported Jews and the Jewish State – may be abandoning that support in favor of unity with those who are blatantly anti-Jewish and anti-Israel.

The call to unity is destructive because cooperation with those who propagate anti-Jewish/anti-Israel propaganda will cause significant damage to strong Jewish-Christian relations based on mutual support for the Jewish State that other organizations have developed over the past decades.

Institutions such as the International Christian Embassy in Jerusalem (ICEJ) have painstakingly built bridges with the Jewish community within Israel and abroad ever since its founding in 1980. Over the past thirty-six years, the ICEJ had earned a solid reputation for its work within Israel and the education of Christians worldwide concerning a biblical understanding of Israel.

But, the foundations for Jewish-Christian relations laid by organizations such as the ICEJ are in danger of being undone through Empowered 21's alliance with Palestinian Christian institutions and leaders who are complicit in the demonization of Jews and the Jewish State.

Where are Empowered21 and Oral Roberts University Headed in Relation to Israel?

Tricia Miller, Ph.D.

This article was originally published in Breaking Israel News on August 17, 2015.

The future stance of Empowered21 (E21) and Oral Roberts University (ORU) towards Israel is uncertain due to the relationship between these two organizations and ORU mega-donor Mart Green. As a result of the $250 million he has contributed since 2008, Green has an inordinate amount of leverage over the perspective of ORU and E21, which is headquartered on the campus of the Christian college in Tulsa, OK.

Green's extensive involvement in both of these organizations in relation to their eventual viewpoint towards Israel is cause for concern because he financed the production of the 2010 anti-Israel documentary, *Little Town of Bethlehem*. This film presents a one-sided and fallacious Palestinian narrative that portrays Israel as a brutal occupier, while ignoring the existential threats facing the state of Israel.

The future stance of Empowered21 (E21) and Oral Roberts University (ORU) towards Israel is uncertain due to the relationship between these two organizations and ORU mega-donor Mart Green.

The absence of any public evidence that indicates Green has changed his beliefs in respect to the Jewish State since the production of the documentary raises the question of just how much he will prejudice the final position ORU and E21 take concerning Israel.

The Relationship between E21, ORU and Mart Green

Empowered21 is a relatively new Christian organization that claims to represent 640,000,000 Evangelical and pentecostal Christians around the globe. Since these Christians constitute the part of Christendom that has historically supported Israel's right to exist and defend itself, the stand this movement takes in relation to Israel will have a significant impact on Christian support for Israel worldwide.

This global movement is the result of an initiative launched in 2008 by the Board of Trustees of Oral Roberts University when the newly formed board, under the leadership of Mardel founder Mart Green, "began work on clarifying the mission of the university for 21st century ministry."

ORU was founded by Oral Roberts, a Pentecostal Methodist evangelist who was a strong supporter of the State of Israel. Before Mart Green formed the new Board of Trustees in 2008, the Board had included pro-Israel activists such as Pastor John Hagee, the founder of the two million strong grassroots movement, Christians United for Israel.

The stand this movement takes in relation to Israel will have a significant impact on Christian support for Israel worldwide.

Green became the chairman of the new board in 2008 in return for the donation of $70 million intended to save the Evangelical Christian school from a financial crisis that included tens of millions of dollars of debt. Mart stepped down as chairman in April 2014 but remains a member of the board, and his father David, CEO/ Founder of the Hobby Lobby retail chain, is a member of ORU's Board of Reference.

Mart Green and the ORU Board of Trustees asked The International Center for Spiritual Renewal in Cleveland TN, then under the leadership of Dr. William "Billy" Wilson, to facilitate the 2008 initiative that inaugurated the Empowered21 movement. At the time, Wilson was also the vice-chair of the ORU Board of Trustees.

Concern over how Green's view of Israel could prejudice the future position ORU and E21 take concerning the Jewish State is heightened by the fact that a few months after Wilson was elected as the new president of ORU, he accepted an invitation to speak at the 2014 anti-Israel Christ at the Checkpoint (CaTC) conference.

On January 31, 2013, this same Board of Trustees elected Billy Wilson as the fourth president of the university. When Wilson assumed the position of president of ORU on July 1, 2013, the E21 initiative went to ORU with him. Consequently, the vision for E21 – initiated by Green in 2008 – has become an integral, if not primary, part of the mission of ORU, and Wilson is both president of ORU and chairman of E21, all as a result of the financial clout of Mart Green.

Concern over how Green's view of Israel could prejudice the future position ORU and E21 take concerning the Jewish State is heightened by the fact that a few months after Wilson was elected as the new president of ORU, he accepted an invitation to speak at the 2014 anti-Israel Christ at the Checkpoint (CaTC) conference sponsored by Bethlehem Bible College (BBC) in Bethlehem, a prominent purveyor of anti-Israel propaganda.

Wilson's involvement in the conference gave the Palestinian movement increased credibility in the evangelical world.

BBC and the biannual conferences it hosts promote a Palestinian version of replacement theology that not only teaches that Christians have replaced Jews in the purposes of God, but rewrites the Bible by making the false historical claim that the Palestinians – not the Jews – are the indigenous people of the land. The logical outworking of this theology is the identification of Jesus as a Palestinian, which is in direct contradiction to the Scriptures these Christians claim to believe.

This erroneous conclusion means that the Palestinian people are the rightful owners of the land, which serves their political agenda very nicely by delegitimizing the existence of the Jewish State. It also works hand-in-hand with Palestinian liberation theology, which depicts Palestinians as victims who need to be liberated from Israeli occupation.

When he spoke in Bethlehem in 2014, Wilson stated that he did not share the Christian Palestinians' belief in replacement theology. However, he did not refute their liberation theology.

Wilson's involvement in the conference gave the Palestinian movement increased credibility in the Evangelical world, and it was a portend of things to come. In May 2015, Jack Sara, the president of Bethlehem Bible College, was an invited participant in E21's Global Congress, which was held in Jerusalem and co-chaired by Wilson.

Throughout the conference in Jerusalem, there was a concerted emphasis on the importance of Christian unity and the need to stand with Palestinian Christians. This suggests that E21 and ORU may become aligned with the Palestinian anti-Jewish, anti-Israel narrative, which is nothing more than a new form of Christian anti-Semitism tailor-made for an Evangelical audience.

Mart Green and the film, *Little Town of Bethlehem*

The potential alignment of E21 and ORU with the erroneous Palestinian narrative becomes even more troubling in light of Mart Green's involvement with anti-Israel activists featured in the 2010 documentary he funded, titled *Little Town of Bethlehem.* The film pretends to provide multiple viewpoints of the Arab-Israeli conflict through the testimony of a Christian, a Muslim and a Jew. But in reality, the film offers a single narrative of Palestinian victimization and Israeli violence that is nothing more than a combination of "anti-Israel activism with a theological backdrop."

Little Town of Bethlehem was produced by EthnoGraphic Media (EGM), which is financed by Green and headquartered in the Green family's Hobby Lobby complex in Oklahoma City, OK. According to its LinkIn profile, EGM is "a revolutionary film and new media group exploring the critical issues of our time...We strive to be catalysts – entry points to social change – through film and grassroot programs."

The potential alignment of E21 and ORU with the erroneous Palestinian narrative becomes even more troubling in light of Mart Green's involvement with anti-Israel activists featured in the 2010 documentary he funded, titled *Little Town of Bethlehem.*

Its Facebook "About" page identifies EGM as a nonprofit organization whose "purpose is to serve by sharing true stories that take on the most difficult subjects...and we do not flinch when it comes to presenting raw subject matter or raising difficult questions." The conflict in the Holy Land is one of the questions mentioned, and in relation to this subject, EGM asks, "Will a nonviolent movement bring lasting peace?"

Mart Green's answer to this question is found in his production of the *Little Town of Bethlehem,* which was advised and assisted by the Holy Land Trust, a Palestinian organization that supports boycotts, divestment and sanctions against Israel, conducts politicized tours that target Evangelical leaders with its anti-Israel, pro-Palestinian propaganda, and is a co-sponsor of the biannual Christ at the Checkpoint conference.

The documentary presents the personal experiences of three men: Sami Awad, an Evangelical Christian leader; Ahmad Al'Azzeh, a Muslim; and Yonatan Shapira, a former Israel Defense Forces pilot. While the involvement of these three presumably provides a Christian, Muslim and Jewish perspective, all three of them tell the same story – that Palestinians are innocent victims of an oppressive Israeli occupation, much like the Roman occupation in the time of Jesus.

Sami Awad is the founder and executive director of the Holy Land Trust (HLT), and is also the son of Bishara Awad, the founder of Bethlehem Bible College. The HLT website states:

> Holy Land Trust exists to lead in creating an environment that fosters understanding, healing, transformation, and empowerment of individuals and communities, locally and globally, to address core challenges that are preventing the achievement of a true and just peace in the Holy Land.

However, Holy Land Trust supports the anti-Israel boycott, divestment and sanctions movement (BDS), which according to the Simon Wiesenthal Center, seeks to destroy Israel by demonizing the Jewish State as a 21st century apartheid regime. This is not an action that promotes "the achievement of a true and just peace in the Holy Land."

Holy Land Trust supports the anti-Israel boycott, divestment and sanctions movement (BDS), which according to the Simon Wiesenthal Center, seeks to destroy Israel by demonizing the Jewish State as a 21st century apartheid regime.

Speaking at the National Leadership Conference for the Vineyard Church in 2009, Awad stated, "We've actually done training in non-violence for Hamas leaders and other militant groups as well." Since Hamas makes it clear in its charter that it intends "to fight the Jews and kill them"and replace Israel with an Islamic state, the only thing Awad's so-called "training" in non-violence does is give Hamas some unwarranted credibility.

Ahmad Al'Azzeh, the Muslim featured in the film, has served as an activities coordinator for HLT and is the field coordinator for "Musicians without Borders," which works in cooperation with HLT. Al'Azzeh is an advocate of a one-state solution, which means the establishment of a Palestinian state through the destruction of the Jewish state.

Al'Azzeh may think a one-state solution will bring about a true and just peace for Palestinians, but the destruction of Israel will most certainly not result in peace or justice for any of its citizens, Jew and non-Jew alike.

The charges of "war crimes" against Israel are all based on "anonymous and unverifiable hearsay 'testimonies.'"

Yonatan Shapira is a former Israeli air force pilot turned anti-Israel activist. He is involved in "Breaking the Silence," an organization that claims to collect the testimonies of disenchanted soldiers who served during the Second Intifada. However, the charges of "war crimes" against Israel are all based on "anonymous and unverifiable hearsay 'testimonies.'"

Shapira is also involved in the BDS movement, and participated in the "Free Gaza" flotilla in 2010 and another flotilla attempt in 2011. These are not the activities of a person who is working towards peace with an existent Jewish State. Rather, as a picture of him demonstrating for "Palestine" shows, they are the activities of someone who is working for a Palestinian state, which as Mahmoud Abbas declared on July 29, 2013, will be *Judenrein*.

In the absence of any public statement from Green that indicates his perspective concerning Israel has changed since the production of the documentary, one has to wonder just how much his negative view of Israel will prejudice the future stance of ORU and E21 towards Israel.

Sami Awad and the Holy Land Trust support the BDS movement and offer training for Hamas, whose reason d'etre is to kill the Jews and replace Israel with an Islamic state.

Ahmad Al'Azzeh works with the HLT and advocates for a one-state solution, which also means the destruction of the Jewish State.

Yonatan Shapiro is involved in an organization that demonizes Israel through unverifiable means, supports BDS, and participates in anti-Israel flotillas.

These are the only testimonies presented in the one-sided, anti-Israel documentary financed by Mart Green.

In light of the fact that *Little Town of Bethlehem* is still advertised on EGM's Facebook page, and in the absence of any public statement from Green that indicates his perspective concerning Israel has changed since the production of the documentary, one has to wonder just how much his negative view of Israel will prejudice the future stance of ORU and E21 towards Israel.

If the involvement of Sami Awad and the screening of *Little Town of Bethlehem* at Empowered21's "Converge21 USA" conference at Regent University in Virginia in 2012, and the inclusion of Jack Sara in Empowered21's Global Congress in Jerusalem in 2015 are any indication, the final position of E21 and ORU will not be good for Israel.

CAMERA Asks Mart Green to Unwind Damage to Israel's Reputation by *Little Town of Bethlehem*

Dexter Van Zile

Note: The following letter was sent to Mart Green, former CEO of Mardel Christian & Education on June 1, 2016. Mardel, who currently serves as Chief Strategy Officer for Hobby Lobby Stores, Inc., produced Little Town of Bethlehem, *a movie that defames the Jewish state while whitewashing the misdeeds of Palestinian leaders. In the letter, CAMERA asks Mart Green to work to undo the damage done to Israel's reputation and to the reputation of American Jews who support Israel by the movie, which was shown to thousands of people at more than 400 venues.*

Following the letter is an in-depth analysis of the movie, which was sent as an enclosure.

Mart Green
Chief Strategy Officer
Hobby Lobby Stores, Inc.

Dear Mart Green:

I write to you on behalf of the Committee for Accuracy in Middle East Reporting in America (CAMERA). CAMERA is a media-monitoring group that promotes complete, fair and accurate coverage of the Middle East with an emphasis on the Arab-Israeli conflict.

We are a grassroots organization with 65,000 members and offices in Boston, Florida, Los Angeles, New York, Washington, D.C. and Jerusalem. CAMERA is a member of the Conference of Presidents of Major American Jewish Organizations. We also work to promote fair and accurate coverage of the Middle East in Spanish-speaking media outlets through Revista de Medio Oriente. We monitor media outlets in Great Britain through UK Media Watch and BBC Watch, and Israeli outlets through Presspectiva.

CAMERA also promotes full and accurate discussion of the Middle East on college and university campuses with our CAMERA on Campus Program. CAMERA staff assists students on 70 campuses in the United States, Canada, the United Kingdom and Israel as they work to counter misinformation about Israel purveyed by agitators who have become increasingly vocal and hostile on the American college scene in recent years.

While the foundational goal of CAMERA's work has been to protect American (and other) audiences from misinformation about the Middle East, our work has taken on increased importance in recent years.

As you should be aware, anti-Israel animus, which has been driven by inaccurate media coverage and propagandistic treatment of the Arab-Israeli conflict, has also promoted hostility toward the Jewish people throughout the world. Inaccurate and distorted coverage of Israel's conflicts with Hamas has prompted increased expressions of antisemitism in Europe. Jews are fleeing the continent in even greater numbers because of violent attacks against synagogues and Jewish-owned businesses motivated in part by virulent expressions of anti-Zionism and antisemitism broadcast by so-called "peace" and "human rights" activists.

Sadly, the problem of anti-Jewish animus has become especially evident on college and university campuses in the United States, a country that historically has been a bulwark against antisemitism. Over the past few years, CAMERA staff who work with college students have heard first-hand stories of Jews being spit on, pushed to the ground, stalked, swarmed and subjected to death threats by anti-Israel activists on college campuses throughout the U.S. Fifteen years ago, it was not like this.

One factor that has contributed to this state of affairs is anti-Zionist propaganda depicting the Jewish state as an evil and monstrous nation singularly responsible for the Arab-Israeli conflict. Jews who support Israel are subjected to mistreatment because of their association with this maligned and beleaguered nation.

This is why I write to you about *Little Town of Bethlehem*, a movie that you produced under the auspices of EGM Media. The 2010 movie, directed by Jim Hanon, was shown in more than 400 venues, including colleges and university campuses, libraries and community centers, despite including errors of fact, material omissions and historical distortions, all of which serve to put Israel and those for whom Israel is their homeland in a defamatory light.

CAMERA cannot draw a direct causal link between the production and wide distribution of *Little Town of Bethlehem*, but we believe that the movie contributes to disdain toward Israel and its Jewish supporters in the minds of its viewers.

Most of the colleges where it was shown were Christian colleges and universities where anti-Jewish violence is unlikely, but on November 13, 2013, it was shown by the California State University Fullerton chapter of Students for Justice in Palestine (SJP).

This is very troubling. SJP is an extreme anti-Israel group that has a well-deserved reputation for promoting hostility toward Jews on college campuses, and CSUF has a well-documented problem with hostility toward Jews on campus as well.

AMCHA Initiative, an organization devoted to countering hostility toward Jews on campus led by Tammi Rossman-Benjamin, wrote a letter about the hostile educational environment at CSUF in 2012. In the letter, dated February 13, 2012, Professor Rossman-Benjamin asks the university's trustees to enforce a resolution that stated "outside speakers brought to the campus will contribute to educational values, that is the pursuit of truth and citizenship values, and not be brought in for propagandizing purposes."

While Professor Rossman-Benjamin's letter does not mention the showing of *LTOB* at CSUF, we believe that it could very well have been included in her correspondence for the movie is emblematic of the anti-Israel propaganda that has engendered hostility toward Jews on college campuses throughout the U.S. It is very possible that other SJP groups on other campuses also showed the film.

We understand that the movie has received a number of awards from local film festivals and praise from numerous Evangelical intellectuals and even Christianity Today, the flagship publication for Evangelical Protestantism in the United States.

These awards and positive reviews do not detract from the concerns we raised in an article published on our website on Nov. 18, 2015. This article, which addressed only some of the problems with *Little Town of Bethlehem*, appears to have been a factor in the Green family's decision to stop selling the movie on Amazon and on Mardel's website.

CAMERA is gratified that new copies of the movie are no longer available for sale, but our message is the same as it was in November 2015: Given the rising tide of antisemitism — which was a problem well before the release of this movie — your decision to produce and distribute this movie was a fundamentally irresponsible act that needs to be corrected.

The decision of the Green family to produce a movie that depicts the Israel-Palestinian conflict (and Israel) in such a distorted manner, raises questions about the worldview the family uses to manage institutions over which it exerts substantial influence, most notably Oral Roberts University, Empowered21 movement and the Museum of the Bible. It is CAMERA's great concern that if left unchallenged, the distorted view of Israel and of its Jewish supporters will manifest themselves in these institutions just as it did in *LTOB*.

In light of the defamatory and incendiary distortions in *LTOB* (detailed in the attached analysis), CAMERA urges you to embark on a campaign to unwind the damage done to the reputation of the Jewish state and the dignity of Jews who claim it as their homeland.

We urge the publication and distribution of a fact sheet that would be sent to all consumers who purchased the movie through online venues. The sheet would include a list of the problems with the movie and the reality as it should have been presented in the film. In addition to sending the sheet to purchasers of the film, it should also be posted on the Internet, specifically on Mardel and EGM's websites, and if possible, Amazon.com's website.

The campaign would include the preparation and distribution of a press release drawing attention to your efforts to correct the record and unwind the damage done by *Little Town of Bethlehem.* This release should be sent to relevant media outlets, including *Christianity Today.*

We also call on you to prepare and distribute an open letter to all the institutions where the film was shown informing them of the problems with the movie and of your desire to correct the record.

We understand these measures are exacting, but believe they are justified and necessary in light of the damaging false messages of the film and the emotional effects it had on thousands of viewers. The movie's propagandistic treatment of the Arab-Israeli conflict incited hostility and unwarranted contempt toward Israel and its Jewish supporters in the minds of thousands of viewers.

If you undertake a campaign to unwind the damage caused by *Little Town of Bethlehem*, it will be an act of great courage and integrity and will also serve as an example of the biblical principle of repentance that is required of leaders.

There is one last issue. *Little Town of Bethlehem* is not the only film that CAMERA is concerned about. Another film, *With God on Our Side* produced by Porter Speakman, Jr. offers a similarly distorted understanding of the Arab-Israeli conflict. Given the thematic similarities between the two films, which were released at about the same time, we feel compelled to ask if the Green family was involved with the production of *With God on Our Side* as well. If the Green family financed the production of *WGOS*, we ask that you embark on a process of unwinding the damage caused by this film as well.

Thank you for your attention to these very serious concerns.

Sincerely,

Dexter Van Zile
Christian Media Analyst
CAMERA
Boston, Massachusetts

CC:David Green
Founder and CEO
Hobby Lobby Stores, Inc.

Steve Green
President
Hobby Lobby Stores, Inc.

Jim Hanon
Writer, Director
Minus Red

In-Depth Analysis of *Little Town of Bethlehem*

In its opening frames, *Little Town of Bethlehem* (*LTOB*) declares that it is dedicated to the emerging non-violence movement in the Holy Land. A close analysis of the film however, indicates that it is not a study or promotion of principled non-violence. Instead it is a deceptive and propagandistic film that serves to excuse and downplay Palestinian violence and hinder Israeli efforts to defend its citizens from attack.

To this end, the movie portrays Israel as an all-powerful, lawless aggressor that is oppressing weak and innocent Palestinians who are merely attempting to achieve their civil rights — just like American blacks in the American south in the 1960s.

LTOB promotes this false and distorted view with the use of misinformation, material omissions and the juxtaposition of images that encourage viewers to see similarities where none exist. The movie also presents distorted reenactments and in one instance, presents footage in a deceptive manner, to lend an unwarranted air of credibility to the narrative it proffers.

To lend further unwarranted credence to the film's narrative, director Jim Hanon combines the testimony of two Palestinians, one a Christian the other a Muslim, (both of whom make false statements about Israel), with that of an Israeli Jew from the left fringe of the political spectrum and totally non-representative of mainstream sentiment, who, instead of defending his country from these falsehoods, affirms them. This combination of sources gives the film an aura of balance that it does not deserve.

Instead of producing a film that promotes peace, director Jim Hanon, has produced a film that promotes what analyst Nidra Poller has termed a "lethal narrative" — a story that obscures Arab and Muslim hostility toward Israel and the Jewish people. Such narratives are lethal because they de-legitimize the Jewish state and legitimize violence against it. That such a narrative was produced under the guise of Christian peacemaking is simply inexcusable. Below is a summary of the problems with the movie.

The movie offers a false equivalence between the Palestinian cause and the civil rights movement in the United States. It also portrays the First Intifada as a non-violent uprising.

Little Town of Bethlehem posits equivalence between Palestinian violence and the civil rights movement in the United States in a number of ways, most notably by juxtaposing footage of the protesters being attacked by Bull Connor's police with images of Palestinians fighting with Israeli soldiers, presumably in the West Bank. To drive the point home, the movie quotes Sami Awad, who asserts "The First Intifada was a lot like the civil rights movement in the U.S."

Elsewhere in the movie, Awad states that Palestinian violence is an attempt by the Palestinians to be treated as equals by the Israelis.

There is simply no equivalence between the civil rights movement in the U.S. and the Palestinian national cause. African Americans were peacefully seeking to achieve their rights under the U.S. Constitution, while Palestinian terrorists in groups like the Popular Front for the Liberation of Palestine (PFLP), Hamas, and Palestinian Islamic Jihad (PIJ) seek to deny the Jewish people their right to self-determination and promote the use of violence to achieve this goal. These groups call both directly and indirectly for the destruction of Israel. Martin Luther King did not pursue the destruction of the American republic, but was calling on its people and government to live and govern by its principles.

The Fatah-dominated Palestinian Authority is basically the same in its constant glorification of terrorism. The PA, which was recognized under the Oslo Accords signed in the early 1990s, has failed to negotiate in good faith with Israeli leaders and has also encouraged violence against Israel.

Moreover, the Palestinian national constitution approved by Palestinian leaders in 2003 declares that Islam is the religion of the state and that Shariah shall be the primary source of legislation.

Shariah enshrines Muslim dominance over non-Muslims, most notably Jews and Christians. Martin Luther King was of course, pursuing equality for American blacks. The Palestinian constitution enshrines Muslim supremacy as a matter of law.

On the more specific issue of Awad's assertion that the First Intifada was "a lot like" the non-violent civil rights movement in the U.S., this assertion ignores one obvious fact: Despite the of-repeated assertion that the First Intifada was a "non-violent" uprising, it was no such thing. Between 1987 and 1992, thousands of firebombs were thrown at Israelis by Palestinian terrorists. Dozens of Israelis were killed by these and other acts of violence during this time.

Moreover, hundreds of Palestinians suspected of collaborating were killed by their fellow Palestinians. The effort to root out suspected collaborators provided a cover for widespread score-settling murders in Palestinian society. This internecine violence is one of the reasons why Palestinian leaders worked to bring the First Intifada to an end.

There were no comparable acts of violence perpetrated by the civil rights movement led by MLK.

To compare the self-disciplined, moral and non-violent civil rights movement in the United States with the First Intifada is an insult to the memory of Rev. Dr. Martin Luther King, Jr. and to the African American community in the United States.

The film posits a false equivalence between Rev. Dr. Martin Luther King, Jr. and Palestinian leaders and agitators who, instead of promoting the rights of their followers, have used their power to delegitimize the Jewish state and undermine the Jewish right to self-determination.

To further the insult against Martin Luther King, *LTOB* posits a false equivalence between him and Mubarak Awad who is well-known for using the language of non-violence as a cover for anti-Israelism.

It does this by juxtaposing testimony about Mubarak Awad with imagery of and speeches delivered by Rev. Dr. Martin Luther King. Viewers are left to draw the inference that Mubarak Awad and MLK are cut from the same ideological and theological cloth, when in fact there is no similarity whatsoever between the two. Awad does not in any sense compare to this great American leader.

In an article published in the Journal of Palestine Studies in 1984, Awad wrote that non-violence "does not rule out the possibility of armed struggle at a later stage." He also wrote that "Non-violence can be successfully utilized, at least in part, by individuals who are not necessarily committed to non-violence and who may choose, at a different stage, to engage in armed struggle."

In this same article, Awad writes that "There is the instinctive need of demonstrators to draw the Israeli army into a confrontation with them. The methods most commonly used presently are to burn tires, throw stones or set up roadblocks." Throwing stones, it must be said, is a potentially lethal activity and simply cannot be considered a tactic of non-violence.

And in 1991 Mubarak Awad said, "I'm willing to go to the soldiers and talk to the fellow with the gun about non-violence. And if it works, I tell him, you won't have to use the gun. And if it doesn't, you can always go back to using the gun. My brother says, 'No, no, no. You can't tell them you can use a gun.'"

Martin Luther King, Jr. would never talk in such cynical terms about nonviolence as Mubarak Awad did in 1991. For MLK, non-violence was not an instrument or a strategy to be used and abandoned as circumstances warranted. In his book, *Martin & Malcolm & America: A Dream or a Nightmare* (2007, Maryknoll), author Rev. James Cone provides the following quote from MLK to highlight his commitment to nonviolence:

"If he beats you, you develop the power to accept it without retaliating. If he doesn't beat you, fine. If he throws you in jail in the process, you go on in there and transform the jail from a dungeon of shame to a haven of freedom and human dignity. Even if he tries to kill you, you develop the quiet courage of dying if necessary without killing."

There's more. In 2002 Mubarak Awad spoke at Princeton University and declared: "I am telling you loud and clear there cannot be a Jewish state in the Middle East. It is impossible."
This is in direct contradiction to what MLK stated multiple times during his career. Martin Luther King, Jr. was an avowed Zionist.

Alex Lubin, author of *Geographies of Liberation: The Making of an Afro-Arab Imaginary* (2014, University of North Carolina Press), reports that in June, 1967, MLK was a signatory to a paid advertisement in the *New York Times* that "called on President Lyndon Johnson to honor

American commitments to ensure Israel's security." Lubin adds that Dr. King wrote a letter to the same paper in which he stated "Israel's right to exist as a state in security is incontestable."

In 1968, Dr. King said the following at the national convention of the Rabbinical Assembly:

> Peace for Israel means security, and we must stand with all our might to protect her right to exist, its territorial integrity and the right to use whatever sea lanes it needs. Israel is one of the great outposts of democracy in the world, and a marvelous example of what can be done, how desert land can be transformed into an oasis of brotherhood and democracy. Peace for Israel means security, and that security must be a reality.

And in 2002, one of MLK's close associates, Representative John Lewis, reported the following:

> During an appearance at Harvard University shortly before his death, a student stood up and asked King to address himself to the issue of Zionism. The question was clearly hostile. King responded, "When people criticize Zionists they mean Jews, you are talking anti-Semitism."

There is simply no way to portray Mubarak Awad as following in the path set by Martin Luther King without insulting Dr. King's memory and violating the trust of the audience. But that is what *Little Town of Bethlehem* does, deceiving and distorting.

In addition to falsely comparing Mubarak Awad to MLK, *LTOB* mischaracterizes Awad's conflict with the state of Israel.

During the film, Sami Awad states the following about his uncle Mubarak:

> It reached the point where my uncle was seen as a threat to the security of Israel. It led him to being arrested and put on trial and deported.

Mubarak Awad was not deported merely because he was seen as a security threat to Israel, but because he no longer qualified for residency in Jerusalem, which under Israeli law, is contingent on the city being the geographical center of one's life.

Israeli stripped Awad of his residency permit after he applied for — and obtained — permanent U.S. residency and then U.S. Citizenship. Application for U.S. citizenship requires that the future citizen intends to reside permanently in the United States. By applying for U.S, citizenship, Awad abandoned his Jerusalem residency.

After returning to Israel as a U.S. Citizen under a tourist visa, he was arrested and deported. Awad challenged his deportation before the Israeli Supreme Court. Awad was not deported from Israel because he was a "security threat" but because he became a U.S. citizen and therefore forfeited his rights to Jerusalem residency.

The film omits crucial facts of history that highlight the challenges would-be peacemakers should confront head-on if they are interested in bringing an end to the Arab-Israeli conflict. The distorted historical narrative offered by *LTOB* obscures Palestinian and Arab violence.

The omissions are numerous and egregious.

• The movie makes no mention of the antisemitism broadcast into Palestinian society (and the greater Middle East) by Haj Amin al Hussein, the Grand Mufti of Jerusalem, one of the leading figures of the Palestinian nationalist cause in the 20th century. The Grand Mufti helped recruit Muslims to serve in the Nazi SS in Bosnia, where nearly all of that country's Jews were killed during the Holocaust. This is a relevant omission because of the manner in which Sami Awad invokes the Holocaust later in the film (discussed below).

• The movie makes no mention of the violence perpetrated against Jews of Palestine by Arabs under the leadership of the Grand Mufti of Jerusalem, Haj Amin Al-Husseini, the leading figure of Palestinian nationalism. Hundreds of Jews were killed in Palestinian riots incited by Husseini in the 1920s and 30s.

• The movie also fails to mention the role the Grand Mufti's alliance with Adolph Hitler and the Nazis during the Holocaust and his singular role in broadcasting Nazi antisemitism into the Middle East through Arabic radio broadcasts.

• *LTOB* makes no mention of the UN's 1947 resolution to establish both a Jewish and an Arab state on the land administered under the British Mandate and that the Jews accepted this resolution and the Arab countries in the Middle East rejected it. With this omission, the movie obscures the fact that the Palestinians could have had a sovereign state of their own decades ago and as a result, could have avoided the suffering that the movie highlights, and blames on Israel.

• The movie makes no mention of the fact that it was the Arabs who attacked first when Israel declared its independence in 1948. The movie allows Sami Awad to describe the beginning of this war with the phrase "war broke out." This obscures the role Arab leaders played in setting the stage for Palestinian and Israeli suffering in the ensuing decades.

• The movie does not inform viewers that when fending off the five Arab armies that attacked the Jewish state in 1948, Israel lost one percent of its population.

• In dealing with the Six Day War in 1967, the movie again allows Sami Awad to describe the war as having "broken out" omitting threats and aggressive acts toward Israel perpetrated by Arab leaders in the months and weeks prior to Israel's attack on Egypt on June 4, 1967.

• The movie also omits Egyptian President Gamal Abdel Nasser's numerous threats to destroy Israel, his decision to kick UN peace keepers out of the Sinai Peninsula and the closure of the Straits of Tiran (an explicit act of war), and the massing of tanks and troops in the Sinai in the weeks prior to the war.

• The film omits the fact that Israel begged Jordan to stay out of the Six Day War and that Jordan ignored these pleas by launching artillery rounds into Jerusalem, prompting an attack from Israel to stop the artillery fire.

• The film makes no mention of the "Three Nos" of Khartoum issued by the Arab League after the Six Day War, in which Arab leaders stated their refusal to negotiate with Israel, make peace with Israel or even recognize the Jewish state.

• The film also makes no mention whatsoever of numerous peace offers made to Palestinian leaders over the years. It makes no reference to the offer made by Ehud Barak at Camp David during the summer of 2000, nor does it mention the Clinton Parameters, which Israel accepted (and the Palestinians rejected) a few months later at Taba. Nor does it mention the offer made by Ehud Olmert to Mahmoud Abbas in 2008, which Abbas ignored. All of these offers represented real opportunities to bring the conflict to an end and to provide the Palestinians with statehood, and *every one of them was refused by Palestinian leaders.*

• The movie makes no reference whatsoever to the ongoing incitement broadcast on official Palestinian TV stations controlled by Hamas and the Palestinian Authority.

• The movie does not highlight the role Palestinian leader Yassir Arafat played in promoting hate and hostility toward Israel and Jews throughout the world during his time as head of the PLO, nor does it show how Arafat planned the Second Intifada even as he was negotiating with the Israelis at Camp David in 2000 while serving as head of the Palestinian Authority. The movie's failure to address Arafat's role in the ongoing conflict is particularly egregious in light of the manner in which it assails Israeli Prime Minister Benjamin Netanyahu (discussed below). The impression viewers are given is that Palestinian leaders are innocent and that Israeli leaders are solely to blame for the conflict.

• *LTOB* also omits any description of the corrupt and oppressive actions perpetrated by both the Palestinian Authority and Hamas against their own people. The movie was produced a few years after Hamas and Fatah engaged in a brief, but exceedingly violent civil war over the control of the Gaza Strip, but there was no mention of this in the film. Why was this omitted?

• Moreover, the film makes no mention of the manner in which Hamas attacked Israel from the Gaza Strip in 2006 and 2008/2009 and created a humanitarian crisis in both Israel and Gaza. Why was this omitted? Is Hamas not worthy of the peacemaking activism lauded in this movie? Is the PA's corruption not worthy of full-throated condemnation?

• In its portrayal of Israel as a creation of European Jews, *LTOB* omits any reference to the approximately 1 million Jews who fled to Israel from Arab and Muslim countries in the years after Israel's creation, fleeing violence and oppression at the hands of their neighbors. Much of this violence was rooted in the hostility promoted by the previously mentioned Palestinian leader Haj Amin al Husseini.

These omissions are particularly egregious in light of comments made by Sami Awad toward the end of the film. He says that he and his fellow peacemakers must ask themselves "What can we do to allow [Israelis] to break the barriers of fear" that prevent them from making peace with the Palestinians.

If Awad and his colleague Ahmed Al Azzeh were serious about reducing the fear of the Israelis, they would present honestly and fairly the threats to Israel, the incitement to hatred and violence against the Jewish state. They would also address the failings of Palestinian leaders in the movie. But these failings are obscured altogether in the film. This is simply outrageous.

Taken together, these omissions, coupled with the manner in which the film demonizes the actions of Israeli leaders, indicates that the movie is not using the rhetoric and language of nonviolence to promote peace, but to de-legitimize Israel. The film is, in short, a salvo in a propaganda war against Israel, not a peacemaking document.

The movie mischaracterizes the history of pre-state Palestine by stating that racism and discrimination were not a problem prior to Israel's creation.

In the movie, Ahmad Al Azzeh reports that his grandparents "used to perceive Jewish (sic) just as neighbors and friends. There weren't any kind of racism or discrimination."
Azzeh's report that there was never any kind of racism or discrimination directed at Jews in Palestine prior to the 1948 War is false. There were some local officials and elites in Palestinian society who were willing to live in relative peace with Jews in Palestine even if they opposed the creation of a Jewish state.

But Haj Amin Al Husseini, the Grand Mufti of Jerusalem who controlled the Arab Higher Committee, intimidated or killed these moderates (who were always few in number) outright in the late 1930s.

Contrary to what Al Azzeh tells the camera, racism and hostility toward Jews was a major factor in Palestinian society. It manifested itself a number of times in Palestinian Arab acts of violence, most especially during the 1929 and 1936 riots.

Sometimes Palestinian Arabs protected their Jewish neighbors during these riots, but not always. Writing in 1961, Howard Morley Sachar recounted the murder of Rabbi Meier Castel, the chairman of the Sephardic community in Hebron. On page 22 of his book, *Aliyah: The Peoples of Israel*, Sachar writes that Castel was "a famous orator in Arabic" and was an "honored guest at Arab banquets and ceremonial affairs. And yet his rapport was not quite enough to save his life" during the 1929 riots:

> As the howling band descended upon the venerable rabbi's home, one of his oldest friends, a Moslem who had been raised in the same courtyard with him, persuaded Meier Castel to give him his key.
>
> "I will guard your home for you," he promised.
>
> Whereupon the Arab unlocked the Castel home to the invaders, and the rabbi was promptly disemboweled.

Al Azzeh's assertion that there was not a problem with racism or discrimination in Palestine prior to Israel's creation is false. The area was aflame with genocidal antisemitism.

LTOB distorts the events leading up to the 1996 election of Israeli Prime Minister Benjamin Netanyahu in a manner that whitewashes Palestinian hostility toward Israel and defames the Israeli electorate.

During the film, Al Azeeh speaks about how the Palestinian people responded to the assassination of Israeli Prime Minister Yitzak Rabin who was killed in November, 1995:

> When Rabin was assassinated, a lot of Palestinian people was sad, sad, very sad. He did all he could when he started to think about peace and they killed him. Read the election. When people elected the most fanatical group to be leaders that means the majority of the population do not want peace. [As Al Azzeh utters this previous sentence, the film shows footage of Israeli Prime Minister Benjamin Netanyahu, who won the 1996 election in Israel.]

In fact, some Palestinians were saddened by Rabin's assassination. But enough of them cheered his death that Yassir Arafat put out a ban on reporting about Palestinians rejoicing in Gaza at Rabin's death, just the same way he instructed reporters to not report about Palestinians rejoicing at the attacks against the United States on September 11, 2001. The day after Rabin was killed the New York Times reported:

> In Lebanon today, a Muslim militant rally in Beirut to mourn the death of a Palestinian guerilla leader turned into a celebration of Mr. Rabin's slaying. Thousands of Lebanese and Palestinian militants chanted, "Death to Israel."
>
> Palestinian guerillas and refugees opposed to the P.L.O. took to the streets of the Ain Hilwe camp in southern Lebanon minutes after hearing news of Mr. Rabin's death, chanting, Rabin is gone! Rabin is gone!" and dancing into this morning. The guerillas fired machine guns and anti-tank rockets skyward.
>
> Palestinian and Muslim Lebanese guerrillas also fired into the night sky in celebration in the Beirut suburbs and other Party of God [Hezbollah] strongholds in Eastern Lebanon.

And two days after Rabin's assassination, Alan Makovsky reported the following about the response to the murder at the Washington Institute for Near East Policy:

> If the official Arab reaction contained some positive elements, some disappointing ones, and some predictably negative ones, there were several unofficial statements and images that reminded Israelis of just how deeply popular hatred runs in some quarters. Terrorist groups were happy, of course, although Ahmad Jibril [the leader for the Popular Front for the Liberation of Palestine] lamented (perhaps not sarcastically) that Rabin was killed by a Jew, not a Palestinian. Hamas said it "congratulates" Palestinians for "the death of one of their worst enemies, a criminal." Perhaps the most ghoulish image was the photograph of Amman-based Hamas spokesman Ibrahim Ghosheh displaying a copy of The Jordan Times headlined "Rabin Assassinated" while grinning broadly.

Al Azzeh's characterization of Benjamin Netanyahu's 1996 electoral victory omits crucial information. He stated that Netanyahu's victory meant "the majority of the population do not want peace." Actually, it's not that they didn't want peace, it's just that they wanted security. On the eve of the election CNN reported the following:

> As Israeli voters cast their ballots for prime minister Wednesday, the fear of more terrorist attacks may strongly influence their choice.
>
> In February and March, militant Islamic suicide bombers killed 59 people in Tel Aviv and Jerusalem. The carnage not only shocked the nation, but it inflicted a severe blow to the re-election hopes of Prime Minister Shimon Peres.
>
> Early in the year, Peres enjoyed a 20 percent lead in opinion polls. On the eve of the election, he holds only a 3 percent lead over Likud Party leader Benjamin Netanyahu.

Al Azzeh portrays Israelis as monsters for electing Benjamin Netanyahu as their Prime Minister in the 1996 election, but makes no mention of the deaths of dozens of people at the hands of Palestinian suicide bombers in the months prior to the election. It was the carnage and wish for safety that helped Netanyahu win the election.

Whether Hanon intended to or not, he allowed Al Azzeh to defame the Israeli electorate in an ugly way. This same movie by the way, excuses and condones the decision of Palestinian voters to elect Hamas, a genocidal power.

The film misinforms its viewers about the relationship between Palestinian violence and unemployment in the West Bank and the Gaza Strip.

In the movie, Sami Awad reports that support for Hamas (a terrorist organization that seeks Israel's destruction) "was at its lowest" when the peace process began. He then asserts that Hamas gained support as a result of a rise of unemployment that took place as the peace process progressed.

Awad states "We became more unemployed during the years of the peace process than at anytime prior to that." He continued, "when unemployment grows, the economic situation becomes more difficult, groups like Hamas are able to fill this gap. They come in with their social programs, their healthcare, their education. They are now providing for the community and that creates popularity."

In sum, the story that Awad tells is that the peace process, which began in 1993, contributed to unemployment in Palestinian society, which in turn gave Hamas an opening and fueled the Second Intifada.

In fact, Palestinian violence led to increased unemployment in the West Bank, not the other way around, as *LTOB* states. Statistics compiled by the World Bank reveal that unemployment *declined* in the West Bank and the Gaza Strip *after* the beginning of the peace process and shot up again with the beginning of the Second Intifada.

Here are unemployment numbers from the World Bank for both the Gaza Strip and the West Bank.

Year Unemployment (Percent)

1991	15
1992	27
1993 (Beginning of Oslo)	26
1994	22
1995	17
1996 (Temporary Closures)	24
1997	20
1998	14
1999	12
2000 (Beginning of Second Intifada)	14
2001	25
2002	31

2003	30
2004	27
2005	26
2006	24
2007	22
2008	26
2009	25
2010	24
2011	21
2012	23
2013	23

These numbers reveal that from 1993 until 1996, unemployment in the West Bank and the Gaza Strip declined. It shot up again in 1996 and then started to decline again until the onset of the Second Intifada at the end of 2000.

Unemployment increased in the West Bank and the Gaza Strip in 1996 as a result of Israeli security measures that prevented Palestinian workers from entering into Israel. The measures were imposed after a series of Hamas-perpetrated suicide attacks (mentioned above) that resulted in the deaths of scores of Israeli civilians. Once the attacks decreased, these measures were eased allowing for an improvement in economic conditions.

This is the story told by Saleh Al Kafri, a researcher from the Palestinian Central Bureau of Statistics, in an undated paper. He reports that after the signing of Oslo I in 1993 "the Palestinian economy became better off" and started to recover from the economic crisis that resulted from the First Intifada. Then, during the 1996 closures, Palestinians were unable to get to work in Israel, but fortunately, this "did not last long, and the political situation became calm and settled **which led to the improvement in the economic situations in 1997 up to 2000."**

Looking at the numbers and the chronology, offered by an official from the Palestinian Bureau of Statistics no less, the reality becomes impossible to deny. Palestinian unemployment increased after periods of Palestinian violence, not the other way around. *LTOB* misinforms its viewers in a significant and egregious way.

Little Town of Bethlehem misleads its viewers about the refugee problem, encouraging them to believe this problem is all Israel's fault.

Little Town of Bethlehem tells a generalized story about Palestinian dislocation through testimony from Ahmad Al Azzeh, a Palestinian Muslim who reports that during Israel's war for Independence in 1948, his grandparents fled from the village of Jibrin and moved to what is now Azzah Refugee Camp near Bethtlehem. "They lived in caves for a year, until 1949," he says.

Later, Azzeh reports that the United Nations housed his grandparents in tents with the expectation that they would be able to go back to their village after 10 days. "Those ten days extended [into] 60 years," he says. "And I still live in Azzah Camp," he says as the opening bars of a rap song titled "Bethlehem Ghetto" plays in the background.

The implication is that the Palestinians living in Bethlehem are suffering from a problem similar to that of African-Americans in American cities.
Azzeh also describes the conditions in stark terms. "I live in a place where violence could be on a daily basis," he says. His testimony continues as follows:

> I live in a very small area. It is 200 meters by 150 [meters]. We are 2,026 people in this area. Forty-eight percent are children between zero to 18 years old. You are allowed to move in and out, but you still have to come back at night and sleep in this prison. When we started we were allowed 900 people in 1949 so we cannot expand widely. So the family that was composed of six or five members is now 20 or 30. The same area, the same house so they have to build second floor, third floor, fourth flour even we have in the camp. No privacy of course.

After Azzeh reports these conditions, testimony from Sami Awad places the blame on Israel for these conditions. He states, "Life was on a continuous basis controlled by the Israeli military."

But as demonstrated below, *Palestinian leaders played a huge role in preventing a humane resolution to the refugee problem.* It was they – not the Israelis – who blocked the construction of bigger homes for the refugees. And it was Arab leaders who started the war that created the crisis in the first place.

Here's the background that *LTOB* failed to give its viewers:

The Palestinian refugee crisis is the result of the 1948 War, which was started by Israel's Arab neighbors who sought its destruction. Arab leaders called on Palestinian Arabs to flee their homes to make room for Israel's destruction. Many of these people *and their descendents* live in refugee camps in Arab countries such as Lebanon and Syria that deny them the rights of citizenship. (Jordan is the only country that has granted refugees citizenship).

Palestinian refugees also live in the West Bank and the Gaza Strip where they are under the control of the Palestinian Authority and Hamas respectively. Israeli officials attempted to build permanent housing for Palestinian refugees after taking possession of these territories during the Six Day War. In 1992, *The Christian Science Monitor* reported the following:

> Numerous efforts have been made to resettle these refugees, but all have failed. In 1950, long before the territories came under Israeli control, UNRWA suggested moving 150,000 of them to Libya, but Egypt objected. In 1951, UNRWA vetoed a plan to move 50,000 Palestinian refugees from the Gaza Strip to Northern Sinai when Egypt refused permission to use the Nile waters to irrigate proposed agricultural settlements. In 1952, Syria rejected UNRWA's initiative to resettle 85,000 refugees in camps in that country. In 1959, UNRWA reported that of the $250 million fund for rehabilitation created in 1950 to provide homes and jobs for the refugees outside of the camps, only $7 million had been spent.
>
> In the early 1970s, Israel initiated what it called the "build your own home" program. A half a dunam of land outside the camps (equal to about an eighth of an acre) was given to Palestinians who then financed the purchase of building materials and, usually with friends, erected a home. Israel provided the infrastructure: sewers, schools, etc. *More than 11,000 camp dwellers were resettled into 10 different neighborhoods*

> *before the PLO, using intimidation tactics, ended the program.* (Emphasis added.)
>
> Israeli authorities say that if people were able to stand up to the PLO and if it had the funds to invest in the infrastructure, within eight years every camp resident could own a single-dwelling home in a clean and uncongested neighborhood.

That's not all. In the face of Israeli efforts to provide the Palestinians with permanent homes, the United Nations, under pressure from Arab and Muslim nations passed two resolutions (one in 1976 and the other in 1979) calling on Israel to stop its efforts to relocate the refugees. One of the resolutions even called on Israel to return Palestinians to their homes in the refugee camps. The goal was to use suffering the refugees as a symbol with which to de-legitimize Israel.

Little Town of Bethlehem assists in the pursuit of this goal. Why?

Significantly, today the PA has controlled Area A in the West Bank for 15 years, and yet Palestinians still live in refugee camps. Why are any of these people still living in such camps?

The movie cynically uses the Holocaust to portray Israelis as unable to make peace with the Palestinians.

During the film, Sami Awad describes a trip he made to Auschwitz and Birkenau, two death camps in Poland. Awad states that he witnessed busloads of Israeli children touring the camps with Israeli guides, and heard them singing the Israeli national anthem. He says:

> The shocking part was to see the language that this guide was using. Not to explain this violent act as an act that happened against the Jewish community in particular, but humanity in general and should not happen to anybody in the world. But presenting this act as "What the Arabs and the Palestinians want to do to us now ... [Here, Awad's voice trails off in shock.]
>
> The children are experiencing one of the most traumatic episodes of their life. So many of them probably have their grandparents or great uncles or aunts killed in this places.

For Awad, the scene was emblematic of "How fear is now planted in our hearts," he said, adding that the message offered to the students on these tours is "Fear the Arabs, fear the Palestinians. Do not trust them. Do not make peace with them."

In his testimony, Awad attempts to acknowledge the Holocaust's impact on the Jewish people while trying to universalize or de-Judaize the horror. When he says that the Holocaust didn't just happen against the Jewish community in particular, but to "humanity in general" he downplays or elides one of the primary causes of World War II and the Holocaust that accompanied it – Nazi Jew-hatred. Hitler's overriding goal was to destroy the Jewish people, whom he regarded as an obstacle and threat to the survival of the German race. Yes, Awad is right, a lot of other people were killed during the Holocaust, but the Jews remained the primary target of the Nazis.

Awad also suggests that Israeli leaders imbue their children with an irrational and unreasonable fear of Palestinians. This suggestion can only pass muster if one ignores well-established facts about Palestinian leaders and society (which, conveniently enough, were omitted from the film).

Hamas continually pledges to destroy Israel and for most of its history, the PLO had embraced this goal as well. And while the Palestinian Authority voted in the 1990s under pressure from the Clinton Administration in the 1990s to remove from its charter a call to destroy Israel, PA have stated in the years since that this vote is no longer in force. There is no current officially available charter of the Palestinian Authority that lacks this passage.

And as stated previously, one of the worse purveyors of Nazi antisemitism into the Arab world was Haj Amin Al-Husseini, the Grand Mufti of Jerusalem and one of the leading figures of the Palestinian cause in the 20th Century. Mahmoud Abbas has, in recent years, described Husseini as a "hero."

If Awad were truly committed to non-violence, he would have confronted this bit of history and called on his fellow Palestinians to repudiate the Grand Mutfi. But he has not. Instead he uses rhetoric to point the finger of blame solely at Israel.

LTOB invokes misleading testimony of Yonatan Shapira, an Israeli soldier who is currently part of "Breaking the Silence," a group of conscientious objectors who have very little credibility or support in Israeli society.

Speaking to the camera, Shapira tells a story of being a young idealistic supporter of the Jewish state and proud of his service as a helicopter pilot in Israel's military. Everything was fine until he experienced a crisis of conscience in 2002 after the death of Asalzh Shehadah at the hands of the Israeli airforce.

> It was after they dropped this one-ton bomb on the house of Aseleh Shehada, killed 15 innocents including nine children and left me with the feeling that I am one of the kids that were killed there, because this naïve Yonatan that really identified with his country, he was killed in a way.

The death of 15 civilians, nine of them children, as the result of an Israeli airstrike, is a tragedy, but it is important to know who Aseleh Shehada was. He was a high-ranking Hamas member who founded the Al Qassam Brigades in the 1980s. By virtue of his position, Shehada was responsible for planning many of the suicide bomb attacks that killed dozens of Israelis in the decade prior to his death. He also advocated the instruction of children in terror attacks. All this gives badly needed context to the attack on Shehadah's home. The man was responsible for the deaths of many Israelis and was a legitimate military target. In light of the circumstances, it seems reasonable, if not necessary, to ask, was Shehadeh using his family as human shields to deter Israeli strikes against him?

It's a reasonable question to ask given that Hamas leaders have boasted of using civilians as human shields.

Shapira also reports that "Israeli society is very, very militaristic." Why do we not see the same level of self-criticism from the Palestinian sources in this film? It's not that Palestinian society is without its problems, but that Palestinians are not free to speak the truth about their leaders, their culture, their laws or their religion.

The film uses reenactments to lend legitimacy to a distorted view of history.

Another troubling aspect of *LTOB* is the director's use of reenactments to lend unwarranted credibility and drama to its intense focus on alleged Israeli power and wrongdoing and innocent Palestinian suffering. Here is a list of the reenacted scenes:

1. The scene of a Jewish family from Eastern Europe lighting a shabbos candle and tilling the ground after arriving in Palestine.

2. The death of Sami Awad's grandfather during the 1948. (This is the most gruesome).

3. Ahmad Al Azzeh's grandparents fleeing their home.

4. Jews taking possession of this home, handling the valuables left behind by Al Azzeh's grandparents.

5. Ahmad Al Azzeh retrieving his television while under fire from Israeli soldiers during the Second Intifada.

Taken together, these images tell a story of Israeli Jews establishing a life for themselves at the expense of innocent Palestinians whose lives are disrupted by Israel's establishment. Interestingly enough, there are no reenactments highlighting the impact of Palestinian violence against Israelis. There are brief references to Palestinian violence, such as footage of a blown up bus shown on the screen, but it is not given the prominence warranted.

During reenactments three and four, Ahmad Al Azzeh speaks about how his grandparents fled their home during an attack by the Haganah and about being forced to take up residence in a refugee camp where Al Azzeh lives today.

As he speaks, the video displays an Arab family picking up its belongings, including rolls of fabric, fleeing their home and locking the door behind them. Subsequent images show Jews moving into the home and taking possession of the belongings that were left behind. Similar events happened to hundreds of thousands of Jews from the Arab world who were driven out and lost all their possessions during and after the 1948 war, but this reality is not even mentioned in the movie.

Not only do the reenactments encourage viewers to view the conflict in a distorted, one-sided manner, one of the reenactments is based on a misleading narrative of what actually happened.

During his opening monologue in which he describes his family history, Sami Awad speaks about the death of his grandfather during Israel's War for Independence in 1948. As Sami tells the story in the movie, his family lived in an area between East and West Jerusalem where the fiercest fighting and shelling took place.

In an effort to protect his family, Awad said, his grandfather (Elias), decided to raise a white flag. "But in his attempt to protect the family, he was shot and killed by a sniper bullet."

Awad continues: "After that, Jewish forces came and kicked my father's family out and my grandmother was left with ... seven grandchildren."

To lend drama to Awad's story, director Jim Hanon shows what happened with footage of a man's body being dragged across a stone floor leaving a trail of blood. After that, a woman and a young child are shown digging a grave with their bare hands and a piece of wood.

A man's lifeless body lays on the ground in a white shroud nearby. It's a gruesome and horrifying spectacle.

The story used as the script for this reenactment is contradicted by other family members who tell a different story.

For example, in his book, *Palestinian Memories: The Story of a Palestinian Mother and Her People*, first published in 2008 and reprinted in 2012, Rev. Alex Awad, Sami's uncle, reports that Elias went outside with others in his family because there was a break in the fighting.

Elias, Alex writes, "decided to step outside the shelter to see if it was safe and if the war was over."

He then reports that Elias was shot by an unknown gunman because "he had forgotten to put on his Red Cross armband which identified him as a hospital worker and a non-combatant."

These are two different stories. Alex Awad reports that Elias was killed while checking if the fighting had ended. Sami states Elias was killed while the fighting was going on.

And while Sami says Elias was killed while trying to display a white flag, his uncle says he was shot because he forgot to wear a Red Cross armband.

Sami's version has much more propaganda value than the one told by his uncle because it presents his grandfather as risking his life for the welfare of his family.

This is not the first time Sami has told a story that differs from the one told by the rest of his family. In 2009, he told a group of Christians at a gathering in Texas that the shot that killed his grandfather came from the Israeli side of the fighting, leading listeners to conclude that it was a Jew who killed Elias. But the family, it turns out, has no definitive proof of who killed Elias.

At the 2014 Christ at the Checkpoint Conference, this writer confronted Sami Awad about the discrepancies in the story he tells about his grandfather's death. His response was revealing: "I've stopped telling that story," Awad said.

The use of reenactments to pass off false stories as real is a grave violation of the audience's trust. Brian Winston, author of *Lies, Damn Lies and Documentaries* (2000, British Film Institute), declares that "those who deliberately create events for the camera out of their imaginations and then pass these off as real, or even as authenticated reconstructions of the real ... are simply common liars. They are to media production what paedophiles are to childcare."

In one instance, *LTOB* misleads viewers by passing off footage of an Australian jet as an Israeli fighter plane.

At various points throughout the film, *LTOB* shows footage of a jet fighter while Yonatan Shapira speaks about serving in Israel's air force. The inference that viewers are encouraged to draw is that the plane in question is an Israeli fighter jet. In fact it is not. A close examination of the footage in question reveals that the plane in question has the name of an Australian fighter pilot whose name and rank and back story can be readily found on the Internet.

This information can only be obtained by looking at the film on a frame-by-frame basis, as

CAMERA has done. Viewers who see the film in a public setting simply will not be able to do this.

Little Town of Bethlehem presents the massacre of 11 Israeli Athletes at the Olympics in Munich in 1972 in a confusing and disjointed manner and frames it with misleading testimony that downplays the role of Palestinians in violent acts against Israelis.

Hanon's reenactment of the death and burial of Elias Awad is particularly offensive when it is compared to how he portrays the attack on Israeli athletes at the 1972 Olympics in Munich, Germany.

The 38-second segment about the Munich attack provides some information about this horrendous attack, albeit in a very disjointed and confused manner. During these 38 seconds, numerous images are flashed across the screen, for one or two seconds at a time – an insufficient amount of time for people to comprehend what is happening. While these images flash ever-so-briefly across the screen, the headline "They're all gone" (referring to the deaths of the athletes in question) is also shown very briefly on the screen. Then after this, there is hard-to-understand footage and audio of Israeli Prime Minister Golda Meir condemning the attack.

The intent of this section is not to give college-age viewers (who were born years after the Munich Massacre and therefore lack any real sense of what is being shown) context and information about this horrible event, but instead to inoculate the movie against the charge of ignoring Palestinian terrorism altogether.

After this confusing segment is displayed, *LTOB* allows Sami Awad to provide misleading testimony. He states: "As a Palestinian, I would say that it is not correct to justify and excuse such acts of violence. But it's also not right to label an entire Palestinian community as terrorist."

Awad then goes on to say the PLO is made up of different factions that each have their own military wings which are sponsored by "some countries." He then states, "The Palestinian community that lives in the West Bank and Gaza was not involved in these acts of violence."

This is very misleading. While many international attacks were perpetrated by PLO terrorists living in Jordan, Lebanon, and Syria during the 1960s and 70s, many terror attacks were perpetrated by Palestinians from the West Bank and the Gaza Strip during this time.

For example, on November 22, 1968, Palestinian terrorists killed 12 people and injured another 55 in a bombing of Jerusalem's Mahanah Yehuda Market. In February of the following year, another bomb injured 29 Israelis at Hebrew University.

Then there is the Zion Square Bombing attack that took place in the center of Jerusalem on July 4, 1975. This bombing, perpetrated by two members from the PLO who lived in the West Bank, killed 13 people, including two children and injured 72. The bomb was left in a refrigerator in a neighborhood filled with people doing their shopping for the upcoming sabbath. For *LTOB* to allow Awad to mislead his audience in such a manner is irresponsible.

LTOB omits important information about how the First Intifada began.

Ahmad Al Azzeh reports that the First Intifada began when "in one incident a few Palestinians were killed by a settler in Gaza. Then it was kind of a revolution." No details about the "incident" are provided to the viewers, leaving them to conclude that the incident that started the uprising was an act of political violence perpetrated by an Israeli. In fact, the "incident" that resulted in the deaths of the Palestinians was not an act of intentional violence but a horrible traffic accident in the Gaza Strip.

The accident took place the day after an Israeli businessman, Shlomo Takal, 45 was murdered at a supermarket in Gaza on Dec. 6, 1987. According to a report issued on that day by the Jewish Telegraphic Agency, Takal "was talking to a shopkeeper when he was stabbed from behind in the back of his neck."

Then on Dec. 7, 1987, an Israeli truck driver crashed into two Palestinian taxis, killing four residents of a refugee camp in the Gaza Strip. Falsely believing that the accident was an attack in revenge for Takal's murder, Palestinian youths engaged in rioting with firebombs and stones.

Instead of telling viewers that the First Intifada was precipitated by a tragic accident, *LTOB* encourages viewers to think it was caused by an intentional act of violence perpetrated by an Israeli settler. This is irresponsible.

The movie uses nativity imagery as a propaganda device to blacken Israel's reputation.

Toward the end of the film, director Jim Hanon presents the story of the birth of Sami Awad's first child in 2002 during a battle in Bethlehem during which Palestinian gunmen took refuge in the Church of the Nativity, where Christians throughout the world memorialize Jesus' birth.

LTOB juxtaposes the story of Mary and Joseph finding shelter with the baby Jesus in a manger, against a dramatic account of Awad and his wife seeking a place for her to give birth. Israeli security measures in response to Palestinian violence almost prevented the couple from reaching an Israeli hospital. In Hanon's framing of the story, the fear and uncertainty surrounding the couple's ultimately successful effort to get into Israel was blamed on Israel instead of Palestinian terrorists who caused the increased security measures.

To encourage viewers to see Israelis as being at fault for the Awads' difficulties in reaching an Israeli hospital, the film displays a computer animation of Mary and Joseph moving across a concrete section of the security barrier. Viewers simply cannot miss the connection. This image is followed by another animation of the Three Magi offering their gifts to baby Jesus. The message is that Israel hindered the birth of Sami's son just as the Romans hindered the birth of baby Jesus in Bethlehem 2,000 years ago.

The conflict between Israel and the Palestinians is tragic enough. The use of the Nativity story, replete with computer graphics, to blacken Israel's reputation is defamatory and indefensible.

Conclusion

The problems with *Little Town of Bethlehem* are numerous and egregious. Every effort must be made to inform its viewers that it is an unreliable film that offers a distorted and inaccurate view of the Israel-Palestinian conflict.

A New Christian Zionism: Understanding Supersessionism and Why It Is Unbiblical

Gerald R. McDermott, Ph.D.

A version of this article was originally published in Providence *(Winter 2016), 56-62 and is used with permission.*

Most of us are familiar with the standard narrative about Christian Zionism. It is allegedly a result of bad exegesis and zany theology. While many scholars concede that the Hebrew Bible is clearly Zionist (that is, that its primary focus is on a covenant with a particular people and land, both called Israel, and the land sometimes called Zion), they typically insist that the New Testament drops this focus on a particular land and people, and replaces it with a universal vision for all peoples across the globe.

These scholars assert that *Eretz Yisrael* (Hebrew for "the land of Israel") is replaced by ge (Greek for "land" or "earth"), the latter of which is usually translated, "the whole 'earth.'" Concern with Jews as Jews is thought to be absent from the New Testament – except to insist that there is no longer any significant difference between Jew and Greek (Gal 3:28). Hence, neither the people nor the land of Israel has any special significance after the resurrection of Jesus Christ.

According to this interpretation, the only ones who advocate a New Testament concern for the particular land and people of Israel are premillennial dispensationalists, whose theology often holds to elaborate schedules of End Time events including a rapture. This approach, which was developed in the late nineteenth and early twentieth centuries, is thought to be the origin and essence of all Christian Zionism.

Yet Christian Zionism is at least eighteen centuries older than dispensationalism. Its vision is rooted in the Hebrew Bible, in which covenant is the central story, and the promise of land to a particular people is at the heart of that covenant.

Zionism in the New Testament

The Jews who wrote the New Testament preserved the vision found in the Hebrew Bible and held on to the prophets' promises that one day Jews would return to the land from all over the world, and establish there a *politeia* (a political entity), which would eventually become a center of blessing for the world.

Anti-Zionists concede that the Old Testament prophets, usually writing from exile, predicted a return to the land. But some of them say these prophecies of return were fulfilled when the Babylonian exiles returned to rebuild Jerusalem toward the end of the sixth century BCE.

However, there is remarkable evidence that Jesus looked to a *future* return and a restored Jerusalem. In Matthew 24 he says that when the Son of Man returns, "all the tribes of the land will mourn," quoting Zechariah's prophecy about the inhabitants of Jerusalem mourning when "the LORD will give salvation to the tents of Judah" (Zech 12:7, 10). Then in Matthew 19:28 Jesus tells his disciples, "in the new world . . . you who have followed me will also sit on twelve thrones, judging the *twelve tribes of Israel.*" James Sanders observed in *Jesus and Judaism* that repeated references to the twelve tribes imply restoration of Israel, particularly in Jerusalem. [1]

The Gospel of Luke records Anna speaking of the baby Jesus "to all who were waiting for the redemption of Jerusalem" (Luke 2:38). It also reports Jesus' expectation that when he returns, Israel will welcome him. He said, "You will not see me again until you say, 'Blessed is he who comes in the name of the Lord'" (Luke 13:34-35). Luke suggests that the return will be in Jerusalem (Luke 21:24-28).

When Jesus' disciples asked Jesus just before his ascension, "Lord, are you at this time going to restore the kingdom to Israel?" (Acts 1:6), Jesus did not challenge their assumption that one day the kingdom would be restored to physical Israel. He simply said the Father had set the date, and they did not need to know it yet. It was these sorts of indications in the Gospels and the book of Acts that caused Oxford historian Markus Bockmuehl to write, "the early Jesus movement evidently continued to focus upon the restoration of Israel's twelve tribes in a new messianic kingdom."[2]

Paul, Peter, and the writer of the book of Revelation had similar expectations. Paul used Isaiah's prophecy of restoration in Isaiah 59 to declare that, "all Israel will be saved" at the end of history, when "the deliverer will come from *Zion,* [and] he will banish ungodliness from *Jacob*" (Rom 11:26). In Acts 3, Peter looked forward to "the times of restoration of all things which God spoke through the mouth of his holy prophets from ancient time" (Ac 3:21). The word Peter uses for "restoration" is the same word (*apokatastasis*) used in the Septuagint (the Greek translation of the Old Testament which the early church used as its Bible) for God's future return of Jews from all over the world to Israel.

In Revelation, the Lamb stands "on Mount Zion" in the final stage of history (14:1), and the new earth is centered in Jerusalem, which has twelve gates named after "the twelve tribes of the sons of Israel" (Rev 21:2, 12). In chapter 11, the nations "trample" upon "the holy city for forty-two months." What city is this? It is the one "where their Lord was crucified" (11:2, 8). This will take place before or during the time when "the kingdom of the world has become the kingdom of our Lord and his Christ" (v. 15). So, in the time of the new heavens and the new earth, that new earth is to be centered in Jerusalem and filled with markers of Jewish presence in the land of Israel.

Paul has long been cast as the apostle to the Gentiles, who supposedly took the focus off Judaism and showed that the gospel was really a universal message for all. It has often been claimed that Paul believed the days of Jewish particularity were over, and the days of non-Jewish universalism had begun. According to this view of Paul's theology, God's covenant with the Jews is finished, and that covenant has been transferred to the Church. God is no longer concerned with the Jews, as they forfeited their covenant when they rejected Jesus as messiah.

Although Paul has been read this way for centuries, his letters tell a different story. In Romans 9 and 11 he laments his fellow Jews who have not accepted Jesus as messiah. He says that they cause him "great sorrow and unceasing anguish" (9:2). Yet he says "the covenants" still

1 James Sanders, *Jesus and Judaism* (Philadelphia: Fortress, 1985), 98.

2 Markus Bockmuehl, *Jewish Law in Gentile Churches: Halakhah and the Beginning of Christian Public Ethics* (Grand Rapids: Baker Academic, 2000), xi.

"belong" to them (9:4), and even though they have become "enemies of the gospel," they still "*are* beloved " because of their "election" which is "irrevocable" (11:28-29).

Galatians is the letter most often used to prove that Paul has dispensed with Jewish law in favor of a Church that has left Israel behind. Yet even here he says the gospel is all about "the blessing of Abraham . . . com[ing] to the Gentiles" (3:14) because "the promises [of blessing] were made to Abraham and to his offspring" (3:16). As Galatians 3:29 says, "If you belong to Christ, then you are Abraham's offspring, heirs according to the promise." In other words, the Christian gospel forms a connection to Israel's history beginning with Abraham, not a separation. This is a marked contrast to supersessionism, which asserts that Israel has been left behind.

We find the same pattern in Revelation, which is usually dated near the end of the first century. John writes that the new earth is centered in Jerusalem, whose twelve gates are inscribed with the names of the twelve tribes of Israel (21:12). It appears, then, that a Zionist vision continued in the New Testament church through at least the end of the first century.

These are only a few of the many indications of Zionism in the New Testament, which is why early Christians continued to expect a future for Israel as a people and land.

Early Church Zionism

Justin Martyr (100-165), one of the best-known second-century Christian writers, expected the millennium to be centered in Jerusalem. Although he was one of the first replacement theologians (thinking that the church replaced Israel in some sense), his vision of the Church's future included a particular city in the particular land of Israel.

Tertullian (160 – c.225) also saw a future for the people and land of Israel. In spite of the fact that he decried "Jews" for their ignorance in putting Jesus to death, and thought that God punished them by tearing "from [their] throat[s] . . . the very land of promise," he believed that they would one day be returned to their land. He believed, "It will be fitting for the Christian to rejoice, and not to grieve, at the restoration of Israel, if it be true, (as it is), that the whole of our hope is intimately united with the remaining expectation of Israel" (*On Modesty*, chap. 8).

A bit later in the third century, the Egyptian bishop Nepos (who according to Robert Wilken, "was a respected and admired Christian leader") foresaw a restoration of Jerusalem and rebuilding of the temple. Millennial teaching was prevalent in that area of third-century Egypt, and had been for a long time, along with, presumably, faith in a restored Israel.[3]

This early church Zionism came screeching to a halt with Origen (184-254), who regarded the relationship between the Jewish messiah and the promise of the land as a zero-sum game. Either one or the other could be fulfilled, not both. In other words, Jerusalem did "not designate a future political center but a spiritual vision of heavenly bliss." When the psalmist said "the meek shall possess the land," Origen thought he meant the "pure land in the pure heaven," not somewhere on planet earth.

Augustine (354-430) was willing to call soil taken from Israel "holy land," but he spiritualized the promises of land in a way similar to Origen's. Once Augustine's amillennial eschatology became accepted in the medieval church, with its assertion that the millennium is simply the rule of Christ through the Church, few medieval thinkers saw a future for the people or land of

3 Robert L. Wilken, *The Land Called Holy: Palestine in Christian History and Thought* (New Haven: Yale University Press, 1992), 76-77, drawing on *Eusebius, The History of the Church* 7.24 and other sources.

Israel. All Old Testament prophecies of future Israel were interpreted to be predictions of the Christian Church that came after the resurrection of Christ.

Reformation Zionism

A return to the plain sense of the biblical text during the Reformation restored Christian belief in a future role for a particular Israel, both as a people and a land. Pietists and Puritans in the sixteenth and seventeenth centuries became convinced from Old Testament prophecies and Paul's writings that Jews would return to their land.

Long before the rise of dispensationalism in the nineteenth century, Protestants in a variety of churches foresaw a role for a particular Zion in times before the End. After the Holocaust and the establishment of Israel in 1948, Catholic and Protestant theologians both recognized from Romans 11 that the rise of the Church did not end God's continuing covenant with Israel. As theologians brought new focus on that covenant, many came to see that the land was integral to it.

Twentieth Christian Zionism

Karl Barth (1886-1968) was among those who were convinced of God's continuing covenant with Israel, and he also recognized the significance of the land as part of that covenant. Barth rejected nearly every distinctive teaching of dispensationalism. For example, he repudiated the notion that the End of Days was yet to come, insisting that it started with the coming of Jesus in the first century. He also refused the interpretation of biblical prophecies – such as the idea that a literal Great Tribulation was to be expected, or that there would be a military battle between particular nations and Israel – as straightforward predictions in a literalistic sense.

But at the same time, Barth thought that these eschatological errors were "errors in the right direction." He respected millenarian attempts to take seriously God's sovereignty over world events, including the appearance of Israel as a nation-state in 1948. This was a "secular parable," as was the rise of socialism in modern history. The sudden reappearance of Israel was a type of resurrection and the Kingdom of God. It was a "little light" that bore witness to the Light of the World in Jesus Christ.

Lev Gillet (1893-1980) was another mid-twentieth-century Christian Zionist. Gillet was a French Catholic who became a Russian Orthodox priest after spending three years with Russians during World War I as a prisoner of war. He urged Christians to realize that Israel has a "privilege" and "priority" to the "birthright" since Jews are the "elder sons" in God's family.

Gillet wrote that Israel is the *corpus mysticum* into which Gentile Christians are grafted. Therefore the earthly problems of Israel are "not outside" for Gentiles. Rather, Christians should make Israel's problems their own. Hence to help a Jew is to help Israel fulfill the "mysterious identity" to which it is called. Zionism is therefore a theological question, which no Christian can ignore.[4] What is this mysterious identity? Gillet said Israel was called to the "sufferings of the servant" in Isaiah, and to somehow reveal the divine power through those sufferings.
If Barth and Gillet were right, then we might see that previous assumptions about Israel's land – that its importance was temporary, like that of the sacrificial system or what Christians have called the "ceremonial law" – were wrong. On closer examination of the biblical text, we might

4 Lev Gillet, *Communion in the Messiah: Studies in the Relationship Between Judaism and Christianity* (Eugene, OR: Wipf and Stock, 1999), 158, 161.

realize that the Mosaic law – with its "ceremonial" commands about worship – was a *sign* of the covenant, but the land was part of the covenant *itself*. In God's very first statement to Abraham, the land was central: "Go from your country and your kindred and your father's house *to the land* that I will show you" (Gen 12:3).

Following Abraham, the land continued to be at the heart of the biblical story. According to biblical scholar, Gerhard von Rad, "Of all the promises made to the patriarchs, it was that of the land that was the most prominent and decisive."[5] Elmer Martens estimated that *eretz* is the fourth most frequent noun or substantive in the Hebrew Bible, and is even more dominant statistically than the idea of covenant.[6]

By my counting, the land (*eretz*) of Israel is either stated or implied more than one thousand times in *Tanach* (the Hebrew Bible). Of the 250 times that covenant (*b'rit*) is mentioned, covenant is either directly or indirectly connected to the land of Israel in 70 percent of those instances. Of the 74 times that *b'rit* appears in Torah, 73 percent of those times (54) include the gift of the land, either explicitly or implicitly. According to the *Dictionary of Biblical Imagery*, "Next to God himself, the longing for land dominates all others [in the Hebrew Bible]."[7]

In other words, when the biblical God calls out a people for himself, he does so in an earthy way, by making the gift of a particular land an integral aspect of that calling.

In spite of the connection between land and covenant, some scholars maintain that the author of the New Testament letter to the Hebrews makes the emphasis on land irrelevant when he asserted that the first covenant had been made obsolete (Heb 8:13). However, other New Testament texts indicate that the mention of the first covenant was a reference to the sacrificial system revealed through Moses, not the explicit gift of land.

The letter to the Hebrews moves directly from its statement of the first covenant being obsolete to a discussion of the tabernacle in the wilderness where "sacrifices are offered that cannot perfect the conscience of the worshiper" (Heb. 9:1-2,9). It is clear from this that by "covenant" the text means the Mosaic covenant, which established the sacrificial system – not the Abrahamic covenant, which included the land.

Indeed, the land was God's principal gift in the master covenant with Abraham in Genesis, and its promise was never revoked. Jesus spoke of "the blood of the covenant" (Matt 26.28; Mk 14.24), suggesting there was only one fundamental (Abrahamic) covenant, and that the Mosaic law was an aspect of, but not the same as, that fundamental covenant. Scripture never puts the land on the same level as Mosaic law.

The promise of land in the Abrahamic covenant was never nullified, but the Hebrew Scriptures make it clear that Israel's *enjoyment* of the land was conditional, and that exile would be the consequence for disobedience of the Mosaic covenant.

But just as the original gift of the land was *un*conditional and forever, so too the return to the land was an unconditional gift of grace. Repentance did not precede it. The scriptures suggest instead that repentance and full spiritual renewal will take place *after* return and restoration. In Ezekiel's vision of the resurrection of the dry bones, God says he will take the people of Israel and "bring them to their own land," and then later "will make them one nation

5 Gerhard von Rad, *The Problem of the Hexateuch and Other Essays* (London: Oliver and Boys, 1966), 79.

6 Elmer A. Martens, *God's Design: A Focus on Old Testament Theology* (Grand Rapids: Baker, 1981), 97-98.

7 *Dictionary of Biblical Imagery*, eds. Leland Ryken, James C. Wilhoit, Tremper Longman III (Downers Grove: InterVarsity Press, 1998), 487-88.

in the land." Then, even later, he "will cleanse them" (Ezek 37:21, 22, 23). So the relationship between Israel and the land is governed by both conditional law and unconditioned promise, and fulfillment of the promise proceeds by stages.

The New Christian Zionism

New Christian Zionists do not believe that the State of Israel is a perfect country, or that it should not be criticized for its failures. They also do not believe that it is necessarily the last Jewish state we will see before the end of days, or that we know the particular timetable or political schema that will come *before* or *in* the final days.

However, these Zionists are convinced that the State of Israel, which includes more than two million non-Jews, is what protects the people of Israel. They also recognize that support for this state and its people is eroding all over the world. Mainline Protestants have withdrawn their support and many Evangelicals are now starting to withdraw their support, using the same faulty arguments of mainline Protestants.

New Christian Zionists recognize that Israel exists in a region of movements and governments bent on its destruction. It is an island of democracy and freedom in a sea of authoritarian and despotic regimes, and needs friends as anti-Semitism rises precipitously around the world. The combination of these prudential reasons with strong theological reasons results in the belief that the people of Israel continue to be significant for the history of redemption, and that the land of Israel continues to be important to God's providential purposes.